# Baby Steps™ to Success

## Vince Lombardi, Jr. &
## John Q. Baucom, Ph.D.

# Baby Steps™ to Success

## Vince Lombardi, Jr. &
## John Q. Baucom, Ph.D.

STARBURST PUBLISHERS

P. O. Box 4123, Lancaster, Pennsylvania 17604

To schedule Author appearances write:
Author Appearances, Starburst Promotions, P.O. Box 4123
Lancaster, Pennsylvania 17604 or call (717) 293-0939.

**Credits:**
Cover by David Marty Design
Unless otherwise noted, or paraphrased by the author, all Scripture quotations are from the King James Version of The Holy Bible.

We, the Publisher and Authors, declare that to the best of our knowledge all material (quoted or not) contained herein is accurate, and we shall not be held liable for the same.

First Printing, September 1997


ISBN: 0-914984-95-0
Library of Congress Catalog Number 96-072370
Printed in the United States of America

# Dedication

TO the memory of Coach Vincent Lombardi and all those who follow his dream.

*We are never going to create a good society; much less a great one, until individual excellence is once more respected and encouraged.*
—Coach Lombardi

# Acknowledgments

The authors wish to thank: Terry Bledsoe for his tremendous help and input. Thanks to Jill Lombardi for her love and patience. Also, the same to Vincent, John, Gina and Joe. Likewise thanks to Harrison Baucom for multiple hours of typing, research, editing, and finding quotes; Carol Rogers for obsessive and compulsive editing; Keppy Baucom for research and quotes; Shannon McKnight for organizing, editing, inspiring, and otherwise supervising; Butch Simpson, Barry Wagner, Ken Martin, Sam Dinacola, and Elaine Perryman for their input; Clairalyn, Jeremy, Benjamin, Valerie, Chip, and Sheri for their help and inspiration.

# Table of Contents

# Preface

HE wasn't given long to become a legend. At thirty-four he was a high school coach in New Jersey. At forty-six he was just one assistant coach among dozens. And at fifty-seven he was gone. But what he did in that time had marked Vince Lombardi as immortal. He flashed across the national consciousness as brightly, and almost as quickly, as a meteor. Like a comet, he left a trail behind him as a signpost for those who follow. In ten years as coach of the Green Bay Packers, his teams won five NFL championships, and the discipline he brought to the practice field became the standard training technique for a generation in sports, business, and life.

He came to Green Bay in 1959, at a time of the Packers' lowest ebb—they had won but a single game the season before—and in two years he took them to the NFL championship game. Moreover, he kept them there, and in the capstone years of his career, 1965-67, Green Bay won three consecutive titles, and the first two Super Bowls besides. This was to be Vince Lombardi's zenith!

In 1968 Lombardi retired as Packer coach while continuing as general manager. The team promptly missed the playoffs. In 1969 he was hired to coach the Washington Redskins. He coached the Redskins to their first winning season in fourteen years. Then on September 3, 1970 just before the start of the 1970 season, Vince Lombardi died. Professional football wasted little time in recognizing his contribution. The following summer, he was inducted into the Pro Football Hall of Fame. Today his name is on the trophy given to the winner of the sport's championship game, the Super Bowl. More importantly, his legendary spirit is shared by virtually every successful person in our society. Now it can be yours.

# More Baby Steps!

*Baby Steps to Success: 52 Vince Lombardi-Inspired ways to make your life Successful.* Vince Lombardi's is one of the most quoted success stories in the history of the world. The same skills that Coach Lombardi used to turn the Green Bay Packers from cellar dwellers to world champions is now available in 52 unique and achievable "baby steps." The same principles that made the Packers "Super Bowl" champions can make you a "Super Bowl" employee, parent or spouse.

Be sure to also read **Little Baby Steps to Success:** *Vince Lombardi-Inspired Motivational Wisdom & Insight to Make Your Life Successful.* This wisdom-filled, pocket-sized collection of the best of Lombardi will help you one small step at a time to get you off the bench and into the game of success.

And here's more of the best-selling *Baby Steps™ Series:*

*Baby Steps to Happiness: 52 Inspiring Ways to Make Your Life Happy.* This unique 52-step approach will enable the reader to focus on small steps that bring practical and proven change. The author encourages the reader to take responsibility for the Happiness that only he can find. Chapter titles, such as, *Have a Reason to Get Out of Bed, Deal with Your Feelings or Become Them, Would You Rather Be Right or Happy?* and *Love To Win More Than You Hate to Lose* give insight and encouragement on the road to happiness.

**Little Baby Steps to Happiness:** *Inspiring Quotes and Affirmations to Make Your Life Happy.* This portable collection of quotes and affirmations from *Baby Steps to Happiness* will encourage Happiness one little footstep at a time. This book is the perfect personal "cheerleader."

See pages 261-264 for more information

# Foreword

THIS book is entitled *Baby Steps to Success*. The subtitle is *52 Vince Lombardi-Inspired Ways to Make Your Life Successful*. You may be one of many people who raise their eyebrows and say, "Lombardi and baby steps? That sounds like a contradiction in terms . . ." At first glance this may appear to be true. Yet anyone who knew Coach Lombardi personally can tell you he may not have called them "baby steps," but he certainly practiced them.

Coach Lombardi believed in reducing things to their simplest form. He developed a reputation for having only a few plays but practicing them tirelessly to the point of perfection. He said football was a matter of blocking and tackling better than your opponent. That's pure baby step thinking. As authors, we have attempted to follow the same formula for winning in the Super Bowl of success.

There are two authors of this book, Vince Lombardi, Jr., and John Baucom. When one author is referring to a personal experience he is identified by his initials at the bottom of the page. Our mutual goal is to help improve your life. What Coach Lombardi accomplished with the Packers was not magic. He applied carefully chosen principles in a consistent way. Likewise, we have attempted to isolate and organize the same principles in this book. You may not be able to turn around the Green Bay Packers. You don't need to. Our goal is to empower you to turn around your own life. You can accomplish for yourself what Coach Lombardi accomplished with the Packers. But it's not easy. You begin your journey now.

---

*There's only one way to succeed in anything, and that is to give it everything. I do, and I demand that my players do.*

—**Coach Lombardi**

## Foreword

WHY baby steps? There are occasions when one "big step" is simply too much. However, there's a more important reason to call them baby steps. When a baby is learning to walk she toddles, teeters, and often "falls down and goes boom." Yet nobody frowns and complains, "You'll never make it. Why don't you give up?" Instead, we applaud and say, "Way to go—good boy or good girl." Each new step is applauded along the way.

The same is true with *Baby Steps to Success*. You will toddle before you walk. You will occasionally fall down and *go boom*. There may be times when you want to give up stepping at all and simply crawl. But as you'll discover later, it's important to surround yourself with the kind of people who will applaud, encourage, and help you get back on track. These steps take practice. When you first learned to walk, you didn't take one step and then start running. You practiced. This book is purposefully designed to follow the same model. Sometimes you'll need to read the same thing over again two or three times. Occasionally you'll find similar ideas stated in different form. The book is purposely written that way—to follow the baby step model.

Each baby step is designed to mean one thing at a superficial level, and something entirely different if you look more deeply. Some of the baby steps are simple, concrete, and to the point. Others contain a staggering degree of depth that could be entire philosophies on their own. It is suggested that you read this book twice. The first time is a preview. Highlight the material you find particularly applicable to you, and spend more time with it later. The second time you read it to master the step. This book is about success, one baby step at a time.

---

*A little and little, collected together, become a great deal; the heap in the barn consists of single grains, and drop and drop make the inundation.*

—Sa'di

## Foreword

IN preparing to write this book we came up with a design that is simple and pragmatic. Each baby step is covered in three paragraphs per page, four pages per chapter. Each page is self-contained and can be read independent of the others. Each four-page baby step is self-contained as well. You can read one page, one baby step, or several baby steps at one time. Or you can stop at any point along the way, place the book down, pick it up later, and continue to read without a disruption in your flow of thought.

The chapters have been organized sequentially. They are divided into what makes sense to the authors. Yet you don't have to read them the way they are structured. You can read them out of sequence if you wish. The material will still be immediately applicable and easily understood. It's designed so that a reader who has never studied "success" can understand each concept along the way. If you have spent substantial time already on this concept you may choose to jump ahead, or skip around. That's fine, the material will still be useful.

Every baby step is written about one specific concept. The concept was chosen because it is one Coach Lombardi demonstrated. We suggest when you find one you really need to focus on, write it down on a small card and carry it around with you. Look at it often. Flash cards—post card size—are available from the authors. They contain graphic illustrations of each particular baby step and will reinforce your learning. Tapes are also available on each baby step. The tapes complement the material in the book. They do not duplicate it. The tapes will also be helpful as you focus on the baby steps. A workbook has also been prepared to compliment each baby step. It includes journal activities, self-help questionnaires and other activities—two pages per step—to clarify each concept presented. See end of foreword for ordering information.

---

*The kingdom of heaven is like a mustard seed, which a man took and planted in his field. Though it is the smallest of all seeds, yet when it grows it is the largest of garden plants and becomes a tree, so that the birds of the air come and perch in its branches.*

**—Matthew 13:31-32** NIV

# Foreword

HOW long would it take you to learn a foreign language? It probably depends on how well you need to learn it. If you needed to learn it to live in a foreign country, it would take a bit longer. To have a conversational knowledge of a foreign language could take as little as a few weeks or months.

You speak your native language, simply because you grew up around it. You listened to it, you practiced it, and ultimately you mastered it. You also learned any particular dialect, accent, or inflection. Short of some impediment, the way you speak has everything to do with where and how you grew up. If you grew up in Japan, even as a child of American parents, you might think, drink, and speak excellent Japanese. Though you appear occidental in your physical features, you are purely Asian in your thinking. In the same way, if you grew up in an unsuccessful environment, you may have learned *not* to achieve extremely well. You may think, dream, and speak excellent mediocrity. But the good news is, you can learn to speak the language of success.

How long will it take? It depends on how long you work. How do you learn it? The same way you learn to speak a foreign language. You listen to tapes, read books, look at flash cards, watch videos, go to seminars, and then visit the foreign country—the place where successful people are. *Baby Steps* is designed to help you accomplish that. Remember, audio cassettes, video cassettes, work books and flash cards are available. You can obtain these by contacting the authors at the address and phone number below. Learning a foreign language is not necessarily easy. Learning success will not necessarily be easy either. The best way to do it is *one baby step at a time*. Remember, what Coach Lombardi did with the Packers was *simple* but not *easy*. We have provided you with 52 *simple* steps. However, the work of it is yours. But the good news is this. If you do the work, you will experience the results. Work one baby step at a time. It's a *baby step on the road to success*.

---

*Human Resource Center*
*7433 Preston Circle*
*Chattanooga, TN 37421*
*(423) 855-5191*

# 1

# The Journey
## of
## Success Begins Now

*The journey of a thousand miles begins with one step.*
—Lao Tze

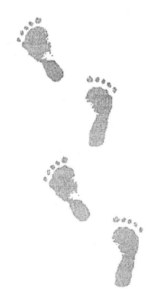

# Success

SUCCESS (suk-ses´) n. 1. The achievement of something desired, planned, or attempted. 2. In ten seasons as an NFL Head Coach (nine with the Green Bay Packers and one with the Washington Redskins) Vince Lombardi's teams compiled a record of 105 wins, 35 losses, and 6 ties. His .740 winning percentage makes Coach Lombardi the winningest coach in NFL history. In eight seasons (1960-67) the Packers played in six World Championships, winning five, including the first two Super Bowls. Coach Lombardi's post season record of nine wins and only one loss is unrivaled in pro football.

Success means different things to different people. Some define success in financial terms. Others define success in terms of power or recognition. Still others would measure it in terms of raising healthy, well-adjusted children. Moreover, your definition might well vary over time, as circumstances work to modify your priorities. At thirty-four years old my picture of success included a Mercedes. I didn't own one, but I wanted one. Twenty years later, given the property we own and our lifestyle, a pickup truck suits me just fine.

So while the definition is personal, there is a simple, singular process for achieving success. It's simple in description, but not in terms of execution. You could read every self-improvement book ever written and be no closer to success than when you began. In fact, more than a few successful people can't read at all! Success isn't in reading. It's in doing. It's in action. It's also in doing and acting on the right ideas. That's the reason we've written this book. Nevertheless, if you don't intend to do the exercises outlined—Stop! Go no further. You're wasting your time. On the other hand, if you will commit to reading this book carefully and keeping a journal, you will find success, however you define it, closer than you ever imagined.—VL, Jr.

---

*If you can't accept losing, you can't win.*

—Coach Lombardi

## Success

LOOK in three different dictionaries. Each might have a different definition for the words "succeed" and "success." If three dictionaries can't agree on a definition, then it's unlikely three people can. The title of this book is *Baby Steps to Success: 52 Lombardi-Inspired Ways to Be Successful.* But a real important question is what we as authors mean by the word success.

The origin of the term comes from the Latin word *succedere.* This means ". . . to follow closely, or go after . . ." Succeed has a similar use today, when you refer to one person "succeeding or following after another." As an example, President Bush was succeeded by President Clinton. That means President Clinton followed in succession after President Bush. Whether either will be considered a "success" in terms of achievement is left up to historians. But we cannot debate the fact that one followed after the other. Our definition of success includes both usages. The first meaning of success refers to "achievement." To be a success, you plan to achieve your goals. The second meaning of success includes the Latin definition of following. This usually means following a plan or set of goals. It may be goals that another person, such as a coach, has helped you make. But it's "following after," the same way President Clinton followed in succession after President Bush. We invite you to follow the formula of Coach Lombardi.

Another twist to the term success is following a well-thought-out plan. Accomplishing an established goal, while losing your family to divorce, is not necessarily success. Neither is achieving in your career, then dying of a stress-induced heart attack in your early forties. Nor would success be defined as embezzling from your company, even though you may be following a plan. Success is something you can experience. It's something over which you do have control. It begins with a plan based on well-chosen ideas. The plan is described in this book. It will place success within your grasp. But only if you follow it and take active steps in the Lombardi tradition.

---

*Folly delights a man who lacks judgment, but a man of understanding keeps a straight course.*
                                              **—Proverbs 15:21** NIV

## Success

ONE of the biggest myths about success needs to be "debunked" very early. Successful people do not achieve at every attempt. In fact, most people who are considered highly successful today have failed far more often than they have "won." One of the most common examples of this comes from baseball. Hank Aaron and Babe Ruth both struck out far more frequently than they got hits or home runs. Thomas Edison failed at his inventions far more often than he succeeded. It's a well known fact that Ray Kroc, Walt Disney, and many other successful people all struggled. And of course, Coach Lombardi and the Green Bay Packers did lose football games.

The fact is, successful people do "fall down and go boom" along the journey through life. They make mistakes. They fail. They get in trouble. They receive bad publicity. They suffer divorces, law suits, and occasional public scorn. If you're attempting to be successful, you won't necessarily be popular. The difference between truly successful people and the rest, is that successful people get back up after falling down. They accept responsibility for their mistakes—whatever they may be. They don't blame the past, their family, or anyone else. They dust themselves off and continue baby stepping through life. They get back on the program. They take a look at their plans and decide how they need to be adjusted. If a change of course is necessary, they make it. They learn from their mistakes, don't repeat them, and continue to march forward.

Success is not necessarily being a talented football player, a billionaire investor, or heavyweight champion of the world. Success is following a well-chosen path and returning to it when you stray off course. And you will stray. All successful people have stumbled. Some gave up and were never heard from again. They couldn't accept failure. However, the truly successful return to their plan. This is what you need to do. Talent is not success. Riches are not success. Beauty is not success. Following the path leading toward a well-chosen goal is. Accept responsibility when you fail. Pay the price. Get back in shape. And return to your plan.

---

*The world can only be grasped by action, not by contemplation. The hand is more important than the eye . . . The hand is the cutting edge of the mind.*
—Jacob Bronowski

Success

COACH Lombardi once said, "Winning is not a part-time thing." In this book success is not a contest or a comet which burns violently and then fizzles out. True success is a way of life. Virtually anyone can achieve in the short-term and then burn out. Remaining on course as a lifestyle is the ultimate achievement. Success, if it is yours, will accompany you everywhere you go—your career, personal, or family life.

Successful people seem to have three key ingredients that help keep them focused. The first is something that is far too uncommon. It's "common sense." Common sense is different from technical knowledge. Common sense means being able to apply knowledge for the good of common people or community. The second ingredient is goal-orientation. Goal-oriented people are driven by key results they want to achieve rather than by impulse. The third ingredient is self-reliance or possessing a high degree of emotional independence. Self-reliant people aren't crushed by the criticism of others. They are independent enough to not give up when others say, "You can't do that!" Each of these qualities is important if you plan for success as a lifestyle.

Take this baby step today. In your success journal, give yourself a personal written assessment of your own strengths and weaknesses in these three areas. Give yourself a report card grade and then write a one-page essay on each factor. Demonstrate *common sense, goal-orientation,* and *self-reliance.* Make plans to strengthen your weaknesses in those three areas, and then act. Let one of your baby steps be to continue reading. You have taken your first baby step. It is one of fifty-two. *The journey of a thousand miles begins with one step.* You've taken that step. You're probably one step ahead of your neighbor. Congratulations. Stay on the path.

---

*No matter what you do, do it to your utmost . . . I always attribute my success . . . to always requiring myself to do my level best, if only in driving a tack in straight.*
—Russell H. Conwell

# Self-Belief

SELF-BELIEF (self bi-leef´) n. 1. The mental act, condition, or habit of developing trust or confidence in yourself. The catalyst that propels you to achieve your dreams and feel worthy of success. 2. When Coach Lombardi arrived in Green Bay, he found a team conscious of its own limitations, secure in its mediocrity, and playing less to win than to avoid embarrassment. The players didn't see themselves as winners. The year before, their record was one victory, one tie, and ten defeats. Into this self-fulfilling prophecy of failure came Lombardi, a strong self-believer, with high self-esteem and resiliency. He transformed his players into champions. He believed in them so they could believe in themselves. Coach Lombardi changed the players' belief system. Because then, and only then, could he begin the task of convincing those players they could be Super Bowl Champions.

No doubt you're familiar with *The Wizard of Oz*. Dorothy is off to see the wizard, the " . . . wonderful wizard of Oz . . . " Along the way, she meets the tin man, the scarecrow, and the cowardly lion. The tin man wants a heart, the scarecrow a brain, and the lion wants courage. But the wizard was a phony who hid behind a curtain. Yet it didn't matter, because the people *believed* in him! Beliefs are that powerful.

The wizard said to the lion, "I know what your problem is, you don't have any medals. Here's a medal. Now you're brave, go out and act that way!" That affirmation by the wizard, who in the lion's mind had magical power, transformed the lion's belief and performance. Change your belief and you will change your performance. Examine your self-beliefs. It's the quality of your beliefs that determines the quality of your life. If you believe, "this is the kind of person I am," that's exactly the person you'll become. This is true whether you believe positively or negatively. If you believe you're worthless, you will become so. And others will treat you as worthless. If you believe you're extremely reliable, stay on that path and you won't need to see "the wizard." You will carry him inside. VL, Jr.

---

*He (Coach Lombardi) made us realize that if the mind was willing, the body can go.*
—**Forrest Gregg**, Green Bay Packers, 1977 Hall of Fame

### Self-Belief

TO achieve, you must first believe. No success is possible without a strong sense of belief in yourself. It is a vital and fundamental foundation without which success is impossible. As with the Packers in the pre-Lombardi era, initially your self-belief may be quite low. Find the seeds of positive self-belief elsewhere. Become infected by other sources of "belief energy." It might be from another person. It might be from this book or from tapes. But begin at the basic belief level. Begin to believe in yourself—even if it comes from outside of you.

You must consider yourself *worthwhile, competent,* and most of all *deserving.* These are the components of self-*belief.* Frankly, most people suffer in each of these areas. Few could sincerely give themselves "A's" on each of these three traits. People with authentic self-belief are uncommon. But the good news is, self-belief can be learned. Coach Lombardi was a genius at communicating these characteristics to his players. He did it through simple repetition. He did it through drama. And sometimes he even communicated it through trauma. But it worked.

The final level of belief has to do with your goals. You need to not only consider yourself but, your goals worthwhile as well. You have to believe in yourself and what you're doing. When you establish belief on all these levels, success is not only possible but likely. Evaluate your self-belief. If you consider yourself weak in any of these areas, comprehensively review the baby steps that apply. Get the flash cards, tapes, and workbook. If you can't find it in yourself, find it in a coach. Without self-belief, nothing is possible. With it, you're on the way to the Super Bowl.

---

*A person under the firm persuasion that he can command resources virtually has them.*

—Livy

## Self-Belief

IN 1976 I ran my first marathon. Looking at me today, some might have difficulty believing I actually completed a marathon. The fact is, I have run over a dozen. Admittedly, the last one was several years ago. But I have actually completed marathons all over the country.

The first one was special. I was on active duty in the Marine Corps and it was the first annual Marine Corps marathon. The course is beautiful. It begins and ends at the Iwo Jima Memorial. For me, as a Marine Corps officer, it was an incredible experience. This was before running marathons was popular. I didn't know anyone who had completed one. I did find a fellow officer who had run track in college and consulted with him. He advised me that it was an achievable goal, but suggested I do it at a very slow pace. He gave me a logical plan to follow, which I did. I completed the marathon in about 3 hours and 45 minutes.

It was actually a pleasant experience for me and I became excited about the possibility of running other marathons. I began reading the few books I could find at the time and became educated. I grew aware of how difficult it was supposed to be. For the first time I read about *hitting the wall,* depletion, and how difficult it is to complete a marathon. Pretty soon I became a believer—or disbeliever. I developed a belief that it was almost impossible. By the time of my next marathon, I had become convinced I couldn't make it—and I didn't! Several months later I re-educated myself. I threw the books away and went back to my simple plan. "I believe I can do this if I go slowly enough—one baby step at a time." My next attempt was successful. I finished the marathon in a little bit over four hours. It was a baby step moment. And I accomplished it because I believed I could. Such is the power of belief.—JB

---

*In order to succeed we must first believe that we can.*
—**Michael Korda**

## Self-Belief

TO succeed on a major level, it's important to develop a deep and profound belief about your own personal destiny. Your belief must be so powerful it transcends presupposed limitations. Most such boundaries are actually products of fear. But if your positive self-belief is deep, fear is irrelevant.

Begin to believe that failure is an impostor. It's only temporary, and it's there for learning and nothing else. Develop the habit of looking on any event which disagrees with you as "school." When you face difficulties ask, "What do I need to learn from this?" When you begin to believe at this level, you're on target. William James said, "Belief affects will." And will changes reality. Today take this baby step. In your success journal, investigate any deep beliefs you have about personal destiny. Answer these questions: "In my deepest most private moments, what do I find to be true about my value, aptitude, and destiny? Do I believe I'm destined for greatness? Do I believe I have the seeds of a champion within me? Do I believe I can accomplish any worthwhile goal that doesn't violate the laws of mankind or nature? Do I believe I am basically a worthwhile person?" If any of your answers fall short, begin developing plans immediately to compensate for these beliefs.

This plan can include various things. Read books suggested in the resource section of this volume. Listen to the audio tapes listed. Use the workbook, tapes, and flash cards. Look on this experience as you would learn to speak a foreign language. You would take classes and listen to tapes. You would study flash cards. You would take risks at trying the new language with others. Eventually you would learn a few phrases. In time you would have a conversational knowledge of the language. If you continued, you would master it. But it would take a while. Learning to be successful will be the same. Begin to believe in yourself today. The only thing you have to lose is your own self-doubt. You will never regret it.

---

*Everything is possible for him who believes.*
—Mark 9:23 NIV

# Vision

VISION (vizh´en) n. 1. The ability to foresee a purpose or goal that appears to be just out of reach. 2. Coach Lombardi had to wait until he was forty-seven years old to become a professional head coach. During the 1950's, professional teams appeared reluctant to hire a New York Italian as head coach. But in that waiting period he didn't fret about missed opportunities. Coach Lombardi spent the time observing, reflecting, learning, and preparing. When he was finally hired to coach the Packers, his vision was clear. He knew precisely what he wanted for his team and how to achieve it.

In the midst of adversity, how do you combat negative feelings and beliefs? You do it through your vision—the clear, precise, vivid picture of success you have created for yourself. In the early stages you alone will be able to see and believe in your vision. Initially it may require more discipline and effort than you think you are capable of putting forth. You may resist committing to your vision. Let what lies beyond the change motivate you. The new and better circumstances you will achieve by changing—your vision. Look beyond current reality. Don't limit your vision by what seems possible today. There's no inspiration in that approach.

Naturally, as a young man my driving ambition was to be in pro football. As a senior in high school, I told my father I wanted to major in physical education because I wanted to coach. His reply was, "That's fine, but if you do, I'll not put one penny toward your education." That was a definite obstacle to my vision! My father was of the generation that wanted their children to be "professionals." So I went to law school, practiced law, and did a number of other things in pursuit of a vision that was not my own. And I was miserable! But I never gave up my vision. I still carry the card where, at the age of thirty-three, I outlined my four step process: 1. The staff of a pro football team. 2. Assistant general manager or in New York working for the NFL League Office. 3. General Manager of a pro football team. 4. Commissioner of the NFL—the vision must look beyond current reality. Within ten years I basically accomplished the first three steps. Then—and this is important—my vision changed. I created a new vision.—VL, Jr.

---

*A man can be as great as he wants to be.*

—Coach Lombardi

Vision
-------

VISION is a necessary component for success of any kind. In fact, all success begins with a *successful* vision. Without it, nothing is accomplished. This is true for your life, but it's also true for specific goals. You not only need to have a life vision, but a project or short-term goal vision as well.

Vision is the ability to understand the present as it currently exists and to simultaneously see a future that grows and improves upon your present reality. It is the imagined grand idea of a bright future. It is *not* a dream. Vision is, in fact, a reality that is yet to come into existence. Vision keeps a person moving in the face of resistance. It overcomes fear, criticism from others, and your own personal doubt. Long after the faint-hearted have given up, those with vision persist. It is the fuel of perseverance.

The kind of vision that high performers possess is palpable, visceral, and real. Your vision needs to be strong enough to fuel your efforts over long hours and, in some cases, many years. By keeping focused on the vision you can make it reality. Vision is your lifetime supply of fuel to keep you on the path. You can experience it in multi-dimensional detail. Make your vision come alive. See, hear, taste, touch, and smell it. Make it specific. Create a vision so powerful that you are surprised when it's not reality. It's an important baby step on the path of success. Remember, vision is not fantasy. It's a future reality you march toward. You have to do the marching. The destination is created by your vision. Visualize to realize.

------

*There is nothing like a dream to create the future. Utopia today, flesh and blood tomorrow.*

—Victor Hugo

## Vision

CARL Sandburg once wrote, ". . . nothing happens unless there is first a dream . . ." I have found myself quoting (or misquoting as the case may be) Sandburg over the past several years during various speaking engagements. While Sandburg's words are poetic, they are also accurate. The dream, however, must be more than that. It must be something you can see, taste, touch, smell, and experience. It needs to be real in your mind, but not quite realized at that point.

Years ago I was helping coach a youth wrestling club which was lucky enough to attend a USA Junior Olympics tournament. (I emphasize more psychological work with young wrestlers than I do physical technique.) This occasion was more the rule than the exception. One particular youngster hadn't been wrestling for very long. Technically he was deficient. However, psychologically his vision was profound. At times it seemed unrealistic. While others would caution him about being overly optimistic, I encouraged him to pursue his dream, which appeared to be out of reach.

He ended up in the finals of his age group and weight class, winning a silver medal. I was more elated with the result than he was. Later he explained that this was what he had anticipated. His vision had been to reach the finals. It didn't include winning them. The following year he changed his vision to winning the gold medal. I thought it was a wise choice. One year later to the week, he won a gold medal. He changed his vision and he changed his reality. He also did the necessary work to make the vision come alive. He then realized the result. The same thing can work with you. Create a powerful vision. Make it just beyond reach. Then act as if it's awaiting you. All you have to do is go through the steps to find it. And you will. Visualize to realize.—JB

---

*Where there is no vision, the people perish.*
—**Proverbs 29:18a**

## Vision

YOUR life vision is a deep overwhelming belief of what your future holds. As stated earlier, it is *not* a dream. Vision is a future reality yet to come into existence. Your life vision is an imagined future composed of the comprehensive results of your life's work. Life vision is a mosaic of your future accomplishments, contributions, and achievements. The more grand and graphic your vision, the more your legacy will resemble it.

To be effective, your vision must be written down in multi-dimensional terms. You need to be able to see, taste, touch, smell, and feel it. You also need to vividly experience it in your mind. You need to visualize the impact you will have in your family, profession, or community. See yourself in multi-dimensional levels—driving the car you will be driving, going places you will be going, and living the lifestyle you have imagined. Put it on paper in vivid and prolific terms.

James Allen said, "Your vision is the promise of what shall one day be." What will someday be for you? What is your life vision? Today take this baby step. In your success journal, write down your *life vision*. Then write down your vision of the next five years. Then write down your vision for four, three, two, and one year from now. Be expansive. Your vision is not a dream. It is reality waiting to be brought into existence. Visualize it. Write it down in graphic detail. Carry it around. Read it daily. Some people go to the extreme of creating a vision of the next three to six months. There's nothing wrong with that approach either. After all, Coach Lombardi's vision was a "winning season," and then another and another. A season is generally three to four months. The same is likely true of every athlete. They have a vision of a successful season. So can you. Develop your vision of success for this season. Convince yourself it can happen. It will. Visualize to realize.

---

*I know of no more encouraging fact than the unquestionable ability of man to elevate his life by a conscious endeavor.*
—**Henry David Thoreau**

# Self-Talk

SELF-TALK (self´ tok) n. 1. The attitudes, emotions, and thoughts you experience during any inner communication—whether subconscious, conscious, or aloud with yourself. 2. Coach Lombardi constantly worked on his players' self-talk with the precision of a skilled surgeon. With each success they experienced together, the players' belief in what Lombardi told them grew. It was reflected in their self- talk. Early in the week, with the mistakes of the previous game fresh in their minds, the self-talk tended to be negative. But as the week progressed and the emphasis shifted toward next Sunday's challenge, Lombardi would become more and more positive. So did the self-talk of his players. By Sunday morning, as a result of Lombardi's influence and their self-talk, and fortified by a history of success together, the players totally believed in their preparation, game plan, and ability to win.

Self-talk is one of the most powerful concepts you will learn on your road to success. Simply put, if you want to succeed, you must understand, internalize, and practice positive self-talk. In reality you engage in self-conversation all the time. When listening, you are actually talking to yourself three times as fast! When the conversation ceases, your self-talk speeds up to four to six times as fast. This is true, even though you may be totally unaware of it.

With self-talk you continually evaluate what is happening in a positive or negative manner. However, it's not what's *happening* that you focus on. It's what you *think* is happening that accumulates into a positive or negative opinion of yourself. It's this internal perception, positive or negative, that controls your behavior. I was first introduced to the concept of self-talk through the landmark book *Psycho-Cybernetics* by Maxwell Maltz, M.D. At the age of twenty-eight I became aware that the same process—self-talk—I had used to form a negative opinion of myself, I could use to create a positive one. If you want to change your behavior, change your self-talk. And don't be afraid of the small losses along the way. They will occur, but with positive self-talk the results will eventually change as well.—VL, Jr.

---

*If we will create something, we must be something. Character is the direct result of mental attitude.*
—Coach Lombardi

## Self-Talk

LIKE it or not, everyone participates in self-talk. You don't have to go out of your way to give yourself affirmations. You are already doing it. They may be *disconfirmation or criticisms,* but you are affirming something constantly. Self-talk occurs when you're asleep or awake, whether you're aware or unaware.

Self-talk is similar to *mental chatter.* It's more important than any skill or gift you possess. And it occurs continually. In fact, during your sleep such self-talk occurs in your dreams. In some ways this is more profound than your waking mental chatter. Yet subconscious self-talk can be controlled as well. You can literally program your "self-talk recorder" to send positive messages.

In *Baby Steps* we suggest you focus on controlling your self-talk. Go out of your way to closely monitor and alter any criticisms or negatives you offer yourself. Self-talk can be a positive way to jump-start yourself out of a slump. At the same time it can be defeating and keep you in the morass. Watch what you say to yourself. It's one of the most important things you can do on the journey to success. Remember, in the absence of a conscious and chosen affirming thought, your mind will usually revert to one of a negative nature. With repetition, positive self-talk can become habitual. But it will take practice. Begin today. Start by repeating to yourself, *I deserve success* and *I'm worthy of success.* Take a small baby step. Do it for one minute at first in the early morning and two minutes at night immediately before you go to bed. It doesn't have to be anything weird. Simply repeat it over and over for a minute or two. Try it for two weeks. You will be well on the road to success.

---

*Our achievements today are but the sum total of the thoughts of yesterday. We are today where the thoughts of yesterday brought us—and we will be tomorrow where the thoughts of today take us.*
—Blaise Pascal

### Self-Talk

BRILLIANT writer and comedian Al Franken had a recurring role on *Saturday Night Live* for years. He also made a movie as the title character in *Stuart Saves His Family*. You got it! I'm talking about the fascinating *Saturday Night Live* character Stuart Smalley who intoned, "You're smart enough. You're good enough. And doggone it, people like you."

Franken, best known for his satire, created Smalley, the "twelve-step" codependent nightmare. In reality we all carry around a little bit of Stuart Smalley inside us. We are constantly affirming or criticizing ourselves. Franken merely stretches the point to make the point. His well-intentioned Smalley struggles to help others while they are often tearing him down. We suggest tearing down no one—especially yourself. And before you attempt to rescue or fix others, take care of yourself.

The critical voice inside your head can be silenced. It can eventually be erased. At first you may need to be as bumbling as the good natured Smalley. Don't be above putting on a baby blue sweater and strutting in front of a mirror, if that's what's required. Incidentally you may want to trade in the sweater for a Green Bay Packer jersey. Or you could put on a crew neck Fordham sweater and a Vince Lombardi era felt hat. Affirm yourself. Coach yourself. You are a winner. You are a champion. And the more quickly you master your own self-talk, the more quickly you will be the master of your own success. Remember, there is nothing esoteric about self-talk. The thoughts are already there anyway. Take charge of them! Begin taking baby steps toward converting them to more positive ideas. If you do, you will change your future.

---

*Your self-image will sustain you in creative living if you learn to declare war on your negative feelings—and win the war in the battlefield of your mind.*

—Dr. Maxwell Maltz

## Self-Talk

YOU probably say things to yourself that you'd criticize someone else for. You allow yourself to get away with verbal abuse of the worst nature. And more importantly, everything you say to yourself is recorded as fact in your subconscious mind. The subconscious cares very little about fact or fantasy.

It's important to become more concerned about self-evaluation than any you receive from others. In the absence of a conscious chosen positive thought, most people will focus on a negative thought. This is due to the continual bombardment of negative input you have probably received throughout your life. Most people are programmed at the deepest of levels to think negatively about themselves. Only with continual monitoring can this be altered.

Look at it this way. There is a war going on. The warfare is inside your own mind. The winner gets control. If you want to win, take this baby step today. For twenty-four hours list in your success journal every negative thought you have about yourself. Take time to note the *where, what, when, why, and how* of the negative or critical thought. You will soon begin to recognize a pattern. You will discover that negative thoughts come at a particular time of day, location, around certain people, or during certain events. There will always be some common element. Often by changing the pattern, you can change the negative thoughts. Then take another approach. Begin to equalize the thoughts on a mathematical basis, one for one. For each negative thought you have, match it with a positive one of equal or greater intensity. It may seem awkward at first, but it will make a difference. If you repeat this habit daily, you will be making giant leaps as you baby step your way to success.

---

*I can do all things through Christ which strengtheneth me.*
                                                —Philippians 4:13

# Examine

EXAMINE (eg-zam´in) v. 1. To inspect, analyze and appraise one's life. 2. Coach Lombardi examined his life within the context of what was most important to him. His religion was most important. It teaches that we have two sides—the good and the evil or the divine and the human. Life is seen as a constant struggle against the dark side. Coach Lombardi's life was partly the public pursuit of excellence. This pursuit earned him fame. He privately struggled against his less admirable qualities. This struggle often humbled him, when upon reflection he knew his actions fell short of his expectations, and the standards he had established for himself. And humility is the sign of true greatness.

A quote in this chapter, attributed to Plato and others reads, "The life which is unexamined is not worth living." If this passage doesn't give you pause, nothing will. You don't have time *not* to engage in periodic examinations of how you are conducting your life. You have the time to develop every quality identified in this book. Just decide what in your life holds a lower priority and give it up.

As a speaker, I spend lots of time on airplanes, in airports, and hotel rooms. It was during these hours that I wrote my part of this book. It has been a time of self-examination for me. You can't write about commitment, faith, love, and hard work without looking inside yourself to see if you walk the talk. This examination has clarified some things for me and prompted me to re-commit myself to important areas of my life. My hope is that this book will help you do the same.—VL, Jr.

---

*Coach Lombardi showed me that by working hard and using my mind, I could overcome my weakness to the point where I could be one of the best.*
　　　——**Bart Starr,** Quarterback Green Bay Packers, Football Hall of Fame 1977

Examine

AMONG my heroes, I include William James, Henry David Thoreau, and Ralph Waldo Emerson. In all my books you'll notice a wide variety of quotes from each of them. They wrote essays and books. They were ahead of their time and insightful beyond belief. I've been told by several people they were all in fact distant cousins. I don't believe genius is necessarily genetic. But in this case, it's probably true.

Each of these men examined their lives. And the world has benefited from their wisdom. This chapter is titled after one of Emerson's essays. The reality is James and Thoreau also spoke about the same topic. Occasionally it's important to truly examine your life. Annually, in fact beginning November 15 of each year, I thoroughly examine my life. I review the current year and look at the one ahead. This process usually takes several days. It occupies an entire ten-hour day on November 15. The following weekends I spend several other periods of time finishing this work.

This annual process is made easier by using a planning system similar to those discussed in the resource section of this book. But it's still incredible and sometimes painful work. Whatever system you use, I highly recommend an annual examination of your life, not only in terms of your goals and plans but also your values and beliefs. Examine your life. It will make it far more worth living. Review your beliefs, values, and goals. Measure how each of them compare with your daily lifestyle and behavior. Be patient. This process takes awhile if you do a good job of it. But it's worth the time, energy, and pain you invest.—JB

---

*The life which is unexamined is not worth living.*

—Plato

## Examine

COACH Lombardi continually examined his life and the life of his team. He looked at every facet of his organization. He took Plato's and Emerson's advice and simplified the Packer's structure and game plan. Coach Lombardi had a limited number of plays compared to the hundreds that other teams used. He kept it simple and practiced his game plan endlessly. Everyone knew what Lombardi was going to do. Yet no one could stop him.

This is the value of examining your life. When I was teaching martial arts, I found many students who wanted to learn different techniques each week. Yet the masters from whom I'd studied didn't count their techniques in numbers. They counted them in quality. They were far more concerned about how well you could do one technique than how many you could demonstrate. This obsession with *quality* over *quantity* is one of the things we all need to examine. Coach Lombardi ran only a few plays but ran them well. The true martial arts masters practice few techniques but can flawlessly execute them. They put years of study into mastering several techniques. This comes from their tendency to examine their lives.

The masters I studied with examined the student's life as well. When you sat for belt examinations, it was a sight to behold. In many systems of martial arts today, hundreds of students can be examined in a three or four hour process by two or three instructors. In my training, five or six masters examined one person at a time. It turned out to be more teaching than testing. There was a lot of pressure. But there was also a great deal of discussion, learning, and compassion. It was a lot of work, but also incredible joy. The unexamined life, on the other hand, probably doesn't experience either range of emotion. It's less work. It's less joy. And it is indeed far less worth living.—JB

------

*Examine yourselves, whether ye be in the faith.*
                                                   **—Corinthians 13:5a**

## Examine

COACH Lombardi, like William James, viewed life to be what you make of it. He had to convince the Packers this was true. They each had to examine their lives, find the shortcomings, and work to overcome them. As they did, life and the results grew more rewarding. But the results only changed because their work changed. And their work changed as a result of self-examination. One of the results of examining your life is believing you may need to change. If you do the work of change your life will improve. However, this only occurs by continuous self-examination.

Like most people, the shortcomings of the Packers had more to do with the way they thought than the way they played football. Coach Lombardi added few players over the years. The people he had were simply those who already were there. It's how he changed their beliefs—not changing the players—that made the difference. He required those around him to examine everything they believed. On several occasions he made the comment that you had to love what you did to be a Green Bay Packer. He said only love would make you pay the price. Yet that in itself was an examination process.

Eventually, as individuals and as a collective group, their lives grew more worth living. They became one of the greatest athletic teams in the history of professional sports. I truly believe it was this continual examination that made the difference. It will make the same difference for you. Examine your life. It will speed you on your way to success. Begin to take this baby step today. Examine your life daily. Look at what you're doing. Try doing things differently. Think not only in terms of improvement, but in meaning. Learn to extract the most out of every living breathing moment you live! This is not a dress rehearsal. It's not practice. It's not drill. This is your *life*. Examine the way you're living. It will make your life far more valuable.

---

*When you have shut your doors, and darkened your room, remember, never to say that you are alone, for you are not alone, but God is within, and your genius is within.*

—Epictetus

# 2

# Finding Your Own Direction to Success

*The ability to concentrate and use your time well is everything if you want to succeed in business—or almost anywhere else for that matter.*

—Lee Iacocca

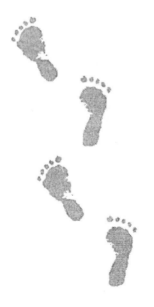

# Life Meaning

LIFE MEANING ( lif me´ning) n. 1. Having a purpose or objective in your life upon which you can anchor your self-motivation and self-discipline. 2. Coach Lombardi loved to deal in the strategies and tactics of football. The task of devising a winning offensive game plan every week totally engaged him from Monday to Thursday. But Lombardi was too complex and complicated to be satisfied with the X's and O's of football. He needed a higher purpose. That purpose was winning, but not so much on a particular Sunday or against a particular team. Winning was a metaphor for life. His players will tell you that three or four times weekly Lombardi would compare football to life. He believed and taught this lesson well. Many former players will assure you that dedication, discipline, focus, and mental toughness led to victory—not only on the football field, but in life as well.

Motivational speakers and authors place special emphasis on goals. I tell groups I speak to, "Without goals we die! Without goals, both personal and professional, we wither and die!" Yet there must be a foundation upon which your goals rest. Without this solid foundation, in the face of adversity you will become sidetracked and your goals will lose their steam. This foundation is your life-purpose and meaning.

Shakespeare said, "Know thyself." Self-knowledge is extremely important. It's been said that all knowledge comes from the questions we ask ourselves. Here's a question I ask myself periodically, "Am I filling my life with daily activities, or do I choose to live my life in accordance with noble principles?" In other words, do I have an overriding purpose in my life? Am I committed to a purpose that undergirds my goals? Or am I avoiding commitments and simply filling my life with daily activities? Ask yourself similar questions. Get focused on a higher meaning. It is a major baby step on the path to success.—VL, Jr.

---

*Unless a man believes in himself and makes a total commitment to his career and puts everything he has into it—his mind, his body, and his life—what is life worth to him? If I were a salesman, I would make this commitment to my company, to the product and most of all, to myself.*
—Coach Lombardi

## Life Meaning

IN 1976 my grandfather decided his life had no more meaning. He described it to me after the Thanksgiving meal of that particular year. Though I objected, he said that at the age of eighty-eight he no longer found meaning in his existence. It was his decision. Three days later he died of "natural causes." At least that was the medical description. He didn't commit suicide. His life had lost meaning and he passed away.

What is the meaning of your life? Sometimes it's difficult to define in concrete terms. Yet it's necessary to investigate meaning in order to experience Lombardi-style success. Your *life* needs to have meaning and so does each specific day. I sometimes carry this to the extreme by saying that each *moment* needs meaning. The meaning may occasionally be inglorious. As an example, the meaning of sleep is to refresh your body. The meaning of a shower is to cleanse your body. Yet without such meaning virtually nothing would happen.

Far too many people live an almost robotic, trance-like existence. They find no meaning and die an early psychological death. Thoreau referred to these people as leading lives of quiet desperation and dying ". . . with a song still in their hearts." This is more often followed by an early physical death. Don't join them. Find meaning in your life. *Carpe diem.* Seize the day. But even more importantly: *Carpe momentum.* Seize the moment. Do so and you will be well on the path to success.—JB

---

*Get into a line that you will find to be of deep personal interest, something you really enjoy spending twelve to fifteen hours a day working at, and the rest of the time thinking about.*
                                                              —Earl Nightingale

## Life Meaning

MANY years ago I was a guest on an after-midnight talk show in Chicago. Something about late hours and the cloak of darkness bring out emotional honesty. The hosts of late night talk shows seem to be a special breed. They are universally bright, articulate, and quite skilled at handling their audience.

The evening had been calm until a particular lady called. She described herself as very depressed and stated she planned to commit suicide that evening if I didn't give her a reason not to. Not only that, she said she was going to do it during the show. To make it more convincing she cocked a pistol near the phone so we could hear she was serious. At first I was shocked and unable to say anything. The host recovered more quickly than I did and engaged the caller in small talk. After a few minutes he began motioning for me to say something.

Finally I was able to talk. I explained, to the caller's surprise, that she couldn't commit suicide because I wanted to meet her the next morning. I suggested that if she killed herself, she would miss her appointment. I told her where I was staying and encouraged her to meet me for breakfast. After a tense few minutes she agreed and promised she wouldn't kill herself that evening. The next morning I went to the restaurant at the agreed time. Not only was she there, but seven other people came as well—all claiming to be her. We had a fascinating therapeutic breakfast. I was able to get her involved in a local church counseling center which helped her. Later she explained that the breakfast appointment was meaningful enough to get her through the evening. She assured me that without such a commitment she would have killed herself during the radio show. Commitment is life-saving and life-sustaining. Meaning is powerful. Build it into your life today.—JB

---

*Be of good courage, and he shall strengthen your heart, all ye that hope in the Lord.*

—Psalm 31:24

## Life Meaning

IT'S common to hear people say depression has robbed their life of meaning. Perhaps it is the other way around. It is not depression that has led to meaninglessness. It is the lack of meaning that has led to the depression! Many times the antidote to a person's depression is simply finding something meaningful to do.

If you find no meaning to your life, there is simply no reason to get out of bed. This emptiness will feed the bowels of deep depression. It actually makes the depression stronger. When you begin to find meaning in your life, the depression is robbed of its fuel. Meaningfulness could be the world's most powerful anti-depressant. It can make drugs as empty as a breath mint.

Today take this baby step. Begin searching for something you can do to help you feel meaningful. If you already have this in your life, congratulations! Expand it and begin to think of your meaning for the next year, and for the next decade of your life. Over time develop an explanation about the meaning of your life. Describe it in detail and discuss it in your *success journal*. Then discuss it with several friends. Refer to it regularly and pursue it with passion. Find meaning in each moment of your life. As a result, your entire existence will be full and rich. You will be living a Super Bowl life. A world championship awaits you, *one baby step at a time*.

---

*The fact remains that the overwhelming majority of people who have become wealthy have become so thanks to work they found profoundly absorbing . . . The long-term study of people reveals that their "luck" arose from accidental dedication they had to an area they enjoyed.*

—Srully Blotnick

# Inner Direction

INNER DIRECTION (in´er di-rek´shun) n. 1. The state of being driven by your beliefs and not by the beliefs of others. The inner-directed drive is so intense that neither people nor circumstances can discourage you from your path. 2. For Coach Lombardi inner direction was a particular asset. He coached during a time when the things he stood for, including the dogged pursuit of excellence, were widely questioned and often repudiated. Consequently, the press often criticized and vilified Lombardi's methods. Did it bother him? Of course it did, especially when the criticism reached the ears of his aged parents, who had trouble understanding the charges leveled at their famous son. While the criticism bothered him, it didn't deter him from continuing on a course he knew was right for him and his players. He had extreme inner-direction.

The opposite of inner-direction is allowing the opinions of others to control you. It makes no difference whether the "others" are specific people in your life or simply your perception of what the community judges to be acceptable. For most of my life I've been outer-directed. Growing up as the son of Vince Lombardi, I was always conscious of people judging me. It was a fishbowl existence. I responded by acting as I thought the son of Vince Lombardi *should* act. It got to the point where I wasn't myself. I became what I perceived other people expected me to be. I have discovered that is no way to live. It's a formula for misery. Attempting to be someone you aren't sucks the life out of you. It's exhausting!

As I grew older I realized that most of the time people weren't watching me. Maybe they were when I was a teenager in Green Bay, but they're not now. What might have been appropriate coping behavior at seventeen is inappropriate at fifty-four. Old habits are hard to break. I'm still working on this one. But the more inner-directed I become, the more liberated I become. So will you.—VL, Jr.

---

*I'm a pretty nice fellow usually . . . they (the press) build me up as a hard man, but I'm not.*

—Coach Lombardi

## Inner Direction

MAKE a study of accomplished people and you will find that every "self-made" successful person is inner-directed. They pay attention to others. However they stay away from those who are overly-critical. At times they may appear impatient. Occasionally they appear to be hyperactive or suffering from ADD. They have a high degree of energy and appear to be conscientiously "on time." They can be described conservatively as gung-ho, and often compulsive to an extreme.

This is not a recommendation to develop Attention Deficit Disorder. However it's important that you begin to nurture the flames of an inner fire. These flames are inner-directed. They come from within. Funnel the energy outward. If you truly want to be successful, you must *act*. Do something. Initiate action. Don't wait for things to happen. Happen to things. You will probably make mistakes. You will likely do some things wrong. But at least you will be doing.

Too many people make the mistake of waiting for others to open doors. If no one is knocking on your door, knock on others. If your phone is not ringing, you need to be making calls. If breaks aren't coming your way, create them. There is no such thing as success "just happening." *You* happen. And success follows. If you wait, success will wait. Let the energy flow outward. When others tell you it can't be done, don't try to persuade them you're right. Just keep on happening to things. Become inner-directed. You may not be popular, but you will be successful. For some people this idea is very difficult to accept. If that's true for you don't despair. Just spend more time on this baby step. Read books from the resource list. Study the concept. Gradually you can transfer your focus to more of an inner direction.

---

*Don't copy the behavior and customs of this world, but be a new and different person with a fresh newness in all you do and think.*
—Romans 12:2 LB

## Inner Direction

WHILE working on this book, I received a call from a friend I worked with years ago in a psychiatric hospital. She is a therapist who was considering the possibility of doing talk radio. Since I am a veteran of talk radio, she was asking my advice. I encouraged her to pursue it. She is a very talented woman who has experienced a great deal of pain in her personal life. With her honesty, compassion, and character I figured she would be a great "hit" and help a lot of people.

Her questioning took an interesting turn when she asked why I took so many "shots" from other helping professionals for doing talk radio. I told her that I didn't know, but my opinion was it would happen to anyone who "colored outside the lines." She laughed at my characterization but agreed with me. Being inner-directed is much like marching to a different drummer. Most people march to one beat—the beat of the status quo. If you are out of step, you 're probably going to be unpopular. It doesn't matter that your step may possibly be more appropriate for you. With most people, if it's different, it's wrong—even if it's more successful.

Artists and inventors have found this to be true. Performers, professional athletes, and high-achievers from all walks of life find the same experience. To do anything out of the ordinary is a sin. To be more successful than ordinary is an unforgivable sin. The Wright brothers were called insane. Marconi was institutionalized against his will. Henry Ford was criticized by others to the point he had to prove his sanity in court. Edison, Einstein, Michelangelo, and virtually all high achievers have had not only their intentions but their mental health questioned. The difference was these people were inner-directed. They did not respond to the opinions of others. Each had developed his own vision and meaning and had the self-discipline to follow his dreams. If you follow a similar path, you can have similar results. Listen to the beat of your own drum. You will be successful.—JB

---

*Whoso would be a man, must be a nonconformist.*
—**Ralph Waldo Emerson**

## Inner Direction

THE biggest challenge to being inner-directed is your tendency to listen to the criticism of others. There will always be someone around who is anxious to point out what you *cannot* do. To the degree you believe them, you will fail. The problem is some of the criticism will come from those you love. Talk to these people and attempt to convert them over as supporters. If they won't change, you have to either learn to ignore them or find new friends.

In your success journal make a list of the people who are encouraging your vision, your meaning, and your goals. If there are fewer than three on that list, begin to recruit more. Send out messages. They will be received. And encouraging people will appear. These are the people whose voices you want to hear. Make a goal to recruit one encouraging voice to match every detracting voice around you.

Make another list of your critics. These are people who discourage, belittle, or criticize your efforts. Stay away from those people to the degree you can. At a minimum learn to ignore them. Don't believe their criticism. And when you can't turn it off or turn it down, block it out. The less you respond to them, the more likely they are to go away. Covet your first list. Encourage these relationships. Ignore the people on your second list. Hopefully their criticism will go away. Once you are baby stepping, companions will appear on the path. Their destination will be similar to yours. As this continues to happen, the critical voices will drop away. Misery loves miserable company. If you're not miserable, they'll find someone who is. It may hurt at first. However, you're better off. Take a risk. Baby step to a different beat.

---

*It is a blessed thing that in every age someone has had the individuality enough and courage enough to stand by his own convictions.*
—Robert G. Ingersoll

# Self-Discipline

SELF-DISCIPLINE (self´dis´a-plin) n. 1. Learning to control your impulses and delay short-term rewards for greater long-range gratification. The ability to keep the big picture in mind while performing the everyday, mundane tasks which ultimately lead to goal achievement. 2. When Coach Lombardi arrived in Green Bay he found players who had talent but lacked self-discipline. They thought they hungered for victory as badly as everybody else in the NFL. Yet they lacked the discipline to translate their talent into success and to do the necessary things to win. It takes tremendous discipline to practice the same play over and over until it becomes automatic. The mastery of any skill requires you to push through the boredom and drudgery that accompanies self-disciplined practice.

If you study the great performers in any field you will discover they all possess one central attribute. It is discipline. However, it's not a tool limited only to performers. We are all in a sense "performers" on our particular stage. If you want to do *it* well, you must do *it* often. "It" is any skill you want to perform as nearly to perfection as humanly possible. Whatever skill or quality you wish to perfect, you must practice tirelessly.

This is where discipline enters the picture. All of us want to "perform" and exit the stage to a standing ovation. The difference between experiencing and only dreaming is discipline. Discipline makes possible the countless hours of practice that leads to mastery. Disciplined people make it look easy. They raise their skill from the conscious to the sub-conscious level. Then they own it. Coach Lombardi often told his players, "Fatigue makes cowards of us all." In part, he was emphasizing the importance of physical conditioning. But there was a more important point. When you face pain and pressure, you will give up your goals unless you have self-discipline. Don't risk it. Work on your own self-discipline. Don't give in to compromise or shortcuts. Self-discipline will lead to a standing ovation.—VL, Jr.

---

*I've never known a man worth his salt who in the long run, deep down in his heart, didn't appreciate the grind, the discipline. There is something good in men that really yearns for discipline.*
—Coach Lombardi

## Self-Discipline

THE dictionary defines the term "self" as the total *essential* being of a person. That's a great definition. The two words that are most appealing are *total* and *essential*. Your *self* is the complete essence of who you are. Sometimes it is difficult to define that self. Your essence and total are difficult to capture in words. But it is important to try.

The term discipline originates from two Latin words. *Discipulus* means "pupil" and *descire* is defined as "to learn." Putting the two together means "to teach." Self-discipline, therefore, is your willingness and ability to teach yourself about the total essence of your being. I also define it as the ability to systematically and progressively work toward a goal until it is achieved. It's doing the right thing, the right way, with the right tools. It is doing those *right things* day after day—week after week—year after year—until your goal is reached. Self-discipline is not easy. It is following your plan religiously. But following that plan and truly developing the total essence of your being is one of the keys on your journey to success.

Initially discipline comes from others. Parents or teachers told you what to do, and you did it. The key is to transfer that externally focused discipline and make it a part of your daily existence. I have often said it's a symptom of self-discipline when you do what you *need* to do rather than what you *want* to do. An even more advanced stage is when what you want and what you need become the same thing. Teach your essential being to systematically plan, pursue, and carry out your goals. You are then self-disciplined and on the road to self-esteem.

---

*Perhaps the most valuable result of all education is the ability to make yourself do the thing you have to do, when it ought to be done, whether you like it or not; it is the first lesson that ought to be learned; and however early a man's training begins, it is probably the last lesson that he learns thoroughly.*

—Thomas Henry Huxley

## Self-Discipline

ELVIS Presley was one of the most talented singers and performers in the history of our country. In fact, the Smithsonian Institution described Elvis Presley as having the most influential impact on the entire history of American music. This man earned over two billion—yes Billion with a "B"—dollars in his brief life. And those were 1950 and 1960 dollars! He was talented. He was wealthy. But he was not self-disciplined.

The total essence of Elvis Presley was ignored. Elvis was driven. He was obsessed with music, career, and success. Someone who knew Elvis explained that he didn't need bodyguards. But he did need lifeguards to protect him from himself. This was true about Elvis. And it's true about a lot of other people as well. Success, as this book has defined it, is not fleeting fame. It involves your total essence.

Elvis's achievements did not come easily. He worked for them. He was not an overnight sensation. He followed many of the strategies discussed in this book, but ignored the most important one. He ignored the total essence of his being. He focused on only one aspect of it. And that was his career. He lost the big picture. Don't make the same mistake. Success does not include dying in your early forties. Begin baby stepping today. Coach Lombardi said success is far more difficult to live with than failure. Success is not having one winning season nor being a big hit and then killing yourself. It's a lifestyle. Elvis will never be replaced. However, *your* premature death can be avoided. Self-discipline will ensure your success over the long haul. Don't let things or other people determine your destiny. Baby step toward your total essence.

---

. . . *the man who masters himself through self-discipline never can be mastered by others.*

—Napoleon Hill

## Self-Discipline

THERE are several elements to true self-discipline. The first is to know the big picture. This includes knowing where you're going as well as how you plan to arrive there. If your goal is to arrive at your achievement level in a body bag, that's one path. If you want to be healthy and arrive with your essence intact, plan another path.

The next step is to find a trail to follow. Study others who have achieved goals similar to the one you are pursuing. Discover what they did and replicate it. Follow the path and the trail blazed by a mentor. The next step is to develop a multi-dimensional vision described earlier. Remember, the more visceral and palpable it is, the more easily you will arrive at your destination. After your vision is written, memorized, and practiced, develop a plan. Produce mid- and short-range goals you want to accomplish. Discover what it is you need to learn or what deficiencies you need to improve. Develop a plan to learn these things. Finally, you must persevere. Persistence and patience are vital to your ultimate success.

Begin this baby step today. In your journal give yourself grades on the qualities described above. If you score lower than a "B" on any of them, you probably need some remediation. Improve your weaknesses. It will speed your way to success. Coach Lombardi would be proud of you. He said, "Our greatest glory was not in never failing but in rising when we fell." This is not easy. Self-discipline is not a natural trait. You will fail. You will get bruised. You will stray. Self-discipline is getting up, brushing yourself off, and returning to practice. Stay with it.

---

*He that hath no rule over his own spirit is like a city that is broken, and without walls.*

—Proverbs 25:28

# Priority

PRIORITY (pri-or´i-te) n. 1. A way of arranging time and activities in order of importance so they coincide with your core values. 2. Football was a major priority in Coach Lombardi's life. However, he constantly strove to keep his coaching career in perspective. He placed emphasis on things he considered more enduring, namely God and his family. Each morning Coach Lombardi attended mass with his wife Marie. This way he spent time with God and his wife on a daily basis.

A favorite quote of mine comes from *First Things First* by Stephen Covey and Rebecca Merrill. "The main thing is to keep the main thing the main thing." What's the main thing in your life? Only a few people can answer this question immediately. Until the question is asked, few think about it. But if you take time, you can come up with an honest answer. Listing priorities is the easy part. Living them is far more difficult. Too often you can confuse important with urgent. Urgent things in life demand immediate attention. They must be done now. Unless you commit and re-commit daily to the important things, you will spend your life overwhelmed by that which is simply urgent.

We're all guilty of this. When I come home after four or five days of travel, the first thing I do is look through the mail piled on my desk. My wife Jill teases that the mail is more important to me than she is. At least I hope she is teasing! In reality, the mail is not more important. However the mail is urgent. There might be checks in the mail! Again we're all guilty of this. My father's priorities were God, family, and the Green Bay Packers. But the week of a big game, he spent most of his time on item number three.—VL, Jr.

---

*Only three things should matter to you: your religion, your family and the Green Bay Packers. In that order.*
—Coach Lombardi

## Priority

IN the movie *Don Juan DeMarco* the writer suggested there were only four questions of importance: ". . . What is sacred? Of what is the spirit made? What is worth living for? What is worth dying for?. . ." You may disagree with the writer. But at a minimum, the observations are deep and profound.

To be a success you must determine your priorities. In this particular movie the writer expressed what was important to her. The important ones for her were those things sacred, spiritual, and worth living or dying for. Each of us has similar criteria. Few people articulate them as poetically. What are your priorities? Can you define what is sacred, spiritual, and worth living or dying for in your life? Frankly, most people can't. The way some react you would think a clean house is the most important thing in life! Or perhaps a good credit rating is! Or maybe jogging for some is their first priority. Few people take the time to look beyond the urgent. Their priorities are actually those that other people have designated for them.

It's not easy to comprehensively list your priorities. At least learn to understand what's important to you. Once you do, you can join the ranks of those on the journey to success. Until you learn to prioritize, you will be constantly distracted and interrupted by trivialities. Incidentally, there was a "right answer" to the "four questions worth asking" mentioned above. The answer to each question was the same. What do you guess she considered the answer to be? In seminars when this point is discussed a number of different responses are given. However, credit rating, career advancement, or a clean house is never suggested. The answer to each question is identical. It is *love*. *Knowing* your priorities is extremely important. You can learn to *live* your priorities by continuing to baby step.

---

*The idea is to make decisions and act on them—to decide what is important to accomplish, to decide how something can best be accomplished, to find time to work at it and to get it done.*
*—Karen Kakascik*

## Priority

I don't have to see movies like *Don Juan DeMarco* to experience drama in my life. I am presented with real life drama daily. On some occasions it's during seminars. At other times it's during intense psychotherapy or on talk shows. Often it's in lively question-and-answer periods after speaking engagements. In fact, I rarely go to see serious movies. I have enough seriousness in my life. What I look for is comic relief.

Yet in many ways I'm lucky because I do get to learn a great deal from others. One of my most successful friends is a corporate trouble-shooter. He's one of the leading corporate turn-around specialists in his industry. On one occasion he told me of a life-changing conversation with his college-age daughter. She had asked him what his priorities were. After hesitating for a moment the answer was, his children, his wife, and his church. Then the dramatic question came, "Then why do you spend eighty hours a week working and maybe twenty minutes a week with us?"

It startled my friend. After stuttering and getting teary-eyed, he told his daughter he would try to spend more time with her. She looked at him for a moment and suggested that she didn't think he would. She explained his actual priorities were where he spent his time. Then she walked away. This was a rude awakening for my friend but he admitted his daughter was telling the truth. He began to bring his *actual* priorities into alignment with his *ideal* priorities. It's never too late. Most people know what their priorities *should* be. The real issue is what they *really* are. Like my friend, you may discover your priorities are not where you want them to be. But you can take action to change them.—JB

---

*And if it seem evil unto you to serve the Lord, choose you this day whom ye will serve; . . . but as for me and my house, we will serve the Lord.*

—Joshua 24:15

Priority

THE first thing to do is to figure out your priorities. Write them down and grow familiar with them. Afterwards, compare your lifestyle with your written ideal priorities. In actuality, living them is the hard part. The massive number of interruptions can sidetrack the most well-intentioned achiever.

The next step is to align your ideal priorities with your behavioral priorities. They need to be so deeply ingrained that they become habitual. When this occurs, you will be able to handle the fires that interrupt you and prevent them from actually overtaking your life. This requires a concerted effort.

Take this baby step today. If you have not done so before, write your priorities in your journal. Most adults actually have between six and twelve priorities. After you write them down list them in order of importance. Coach Lombardi described "Religion, family, and the Green Bay Packers" as his priorities and encouraged them to be those of everybody on the team. He not only had priorities. He had them in order. Like many of us, it was difficult for Coach Lombardi to live those priorities. But he gave it a good try. You can do the same. Figure out the order of your priorities. Then define what each priority means to you and how it will be reflected in your daily life. Remember, it's important to write your priorities down and rank them. Contemplating and discussing them will help. But listing them on paper and defining what each means to you is an invaluable process. Your priorities will likely change from year to year. Go through this process annually. Then let your goals flow from your priorities. Your daily plan needs to reflect your goals. Follow this plan and you'll be well on the road to success.

---

*Set priorities for your goals . . . A major part of successful living lies in the ability to put first things first. Indeed, the reason most major goals are not achieved is that we spend our time doing second things first.*
                                                      —Robert J. McKain

# Time Management

TIME MANAGEMENT (tim man´ij-ment) 1. The ability to use your personal time productively to the maximum possible efficiency. 2. Coach Lombardi was featured in one of the most successful sales motivational films ever produced, *Second Effort*. Made over twenty years ago, it's still popular with sales groups. In the film, Lombardi takes a young salesman under his wing and imparts to him his keys of success. One of the keys is, "Operate on Lombardi time!" If a meeting was scheduled to start at 9 a.m., the Packer players knew they needed to be in their seats at 8:50. If they walked into the meeting at 8:55 they were 5 minutes late.

Every successful person I've ever come in contact with is keenly aware of how precious time is. Some extremely successful people have a secretary or administrative assistant manage their time. That's a luxury most people don't have. So you must rely on a system to manage your time. You don't want to become so compulsively punctual you race trains to be on time for a meeting. Yet how you manage time is an indication of the type of person you are. If you're constantly late for meetings, forgetting appointments and regularly missing deadlines, it sends a message to the people around you. It says you don't respect them, because you don't respect their time. If you did, you'd be on time.

I'm a time management junkie. There isn't a day planner or a sophisticated to-do list I haven't tried. All of them are good if you commit yourself to using them correctly and faithfully. You must strike a balance between controlling your time and having your time management system control you. With your priorities foremost in your mind, plan each day. There will be urgent things that need your attention. In addition, provide time for the important things. Scheduling a specific time for important things, like dinner with your spouse or a movie with your son or daughter, reinforces your commitment to what's truly important in your life.—VL, Jr.

---

*I believe a man should be on time, not a minute late, not ten seconds late . . . I believe that a man who's late for meetings or for the bus won't run his pass routes right. He'll be sloppy.*
—Coach Lombardi

## Time Management

CONTROL is not a dirty word. In this particular context it is a quality that successful people seek. However successful people focus on things over which they truly have control. Less successful people waste energy on things which are uncontrollable.

A good example of this comes from occupational studies. The person who actually has the least stressful job in the country is a symphony orchestra conductor. This is because he has the one thing that is required to lead a stress-free life. He has complete control over his environment. When he raises his baton people respond. That is control. But his is one of the few positions that exacts such privilege. However, when that conductor goes home, just like the rest of us, he gets on the interstate and his sense of control is lost.

In the movie *Falling Down*, Michael Douglas portrayed a man who had virtually lost control over everything in his life. His home, his family, and his job were gone. Eventually he loses control of the only thing he has left— his sanity. Toward the end of the movie the character, portrayed brilliantly by Douglas, poetically arranges for his own death. Though the screen writers resorted to melodrama to make the point, it actually happens to people daily. They fail to focus on the one thing they can control. That singular quality is their own personal lives. Instead, less successful people grow obsessed and enraged over those things that defy them. They grow violent in traffic jams. They scream and curse at TV weathermen. Their mood fluctuates drastically with the rise and fall of the Dow Jones or the win-loss record of their favorite team. That was the mistake of Douglas' character in the movie. You can't control your spouse, employer, the Cowboys, or the economy. Control yourself. And you're well on the way to success.

---

*Lost, yesterday, somewhere between sunrise and sunset, two golden hours, each set with sixty diamond minutes. No reward is offered for they are gone forever.*

—Horace Mann

## Time Management

SEVERAL years ago I gave a friend a day planner for Christmas. We have a very honest relationship and he thanked me for the gift. He stated, however, that he wasn't sure he really wanted to use it. He said he didn't want to become a slave to a schedule. He described himself as a very creative person and felt the use of a day planner would lower his creativity.

This resulted in a discussion that ultimately lasted several days. I ended up conducting a time management seminar for my friend and his business partners. During the seminar I made the point that you can't kill or waste time. You can only kill or waste opportunity. Daily, each person has the same amount of time. The difference between successful people and those who simply want to be successful is filling the time with opportunity. Unsuccessful people don't do that. Time passes, and life happens. To be successful you must make the most out of the time you have available.

The best way to ensure a sense of control in your life is through a time management tool. This can be a day planner, laptop computer with a time management program or in some instances a pocket calendar. Combined with a comprehensive time management seminar it can not only help you get control of your time but ensure progress toward your goal. You don't become a slave to a time management tool. It becomes an ally on your journey toward success. Remember it only works if you use it. Additionally, without a seminar or series of tapes, your time management program can become an expensive "to do" list. Avoid that by using a system that works for you and getting the necessary training to make the most of it.—JB

---

*Know the true value of time; snatch, seize, and enjoy every moment of it. No idleness, no laziness, no procrastination: never put off till tomorrow what you can do today.*

—**Lord Chesterfield**

## Time Management

CONTRARY to popular opinion, successful people don't have more time than others. Everyone has the same amount of time. It is what successful people do with their time that makes the major difference. Simply put, successful people seem to have more control over their lives because they manage priorities, events, and opportunities in the time they have available.

Outside of a few exceptions it's almost impossible to experience success without planning and using a time management tool. However it's not purchasing one that makes a difference. It's using it. Learning to use it is best accomplished by investing in a one or two-day seminar on the subject. The money and time you invest will be returned at an incredible pay-off ratio. It doesn't take time to plan. It gives you more time. People who say they don't have time to use a day planner don't understand. You can't have time *not* to use one.

Japanese time management experts have found if you use time management skills effectively you get an eight-to-one return ratio on time spent planning. For every ten minutes you spend planning, you are rewarded with an extra eighty minutes. German time management experts estimate a twelve-to-one ratio. Any system you buy is well worth the time spent. Take this baby step today. Buy a book or, better yet, purchase cassettes on time management. Experiment with various time management tools until you find one that suits you. Then use it as an experiment for two weeks. Make a decision. Have you become a slave to it or have you become a master of your time? Then find an excellent time-management seminar and enroll in it. Start today. It's a baby step on the road to success.

---

*To every thing there is a season, and a time to every purpose under heaven.*

—Ecclesiastes 3:1

# 3

# Planning Your Keys
# to
# Success

*The key to success isn't much good until one discovers the right lock to insert it in.*

—Tehi Hsiea

# Goals

GOALS (gols) n. 1. Small attainable objectives with time frames leading toward the attainment of your life purpose. 2. Coach Lombardi understood that winning the Super Bowl was the last in a series of goal achievements. The goals can be broken down to each game, every individual player and even to each play. He preached to his players that most games are won by a few specific plays. Since they didn't know which play was going to win the game, the players had to give 100 percent on every play. Coach Lombardi understood that the goal of winning the Super Bowl was built on each player achieving his specific goal on each individual play.

There can be no success without goals. The things we discuss in this book are meaningless without goals. Goals are the alpha and omega of success. You begin your success journey with a goal in mind. On the way you have short-term goals that act as guideposts for your journey. Achieving your short-term goals gives you assurance and encouragement that you are on the right track. As you are about to accomplish a goal, set another one. If you accomplish one without another on the horizon, you risk bottoming out. Goals give you energy. Championships are often won by the more experienced team. One reason is that the less experienced team set a goal to be in the championship game. They've accomplished their goal by just being in the game and they lack the fire to win it. The more experienced team understands this, and their goal is to win, not just participate in the game.

We are by nature teleological. That is, we are goal-striving beings. You need to be committed to clear, vivid, and precise individual goals. If not you will adopt someone else's goals and pursue them. It may be what your parents want, or what you saw on TV last night or read in the latest business bestseller. There is nothing worse than to be out there hustling and striving, not for goals that are important to you, but for somebody else's goals. There's nothing worse. —VL, Jr.

---

*Once you have established the goals you want and the price you're willing to pay, you can ignore the minor hurts, the opponent's pressure and temporary failures.*

**—Coach Lombardi**

Goals

THEODORE Roosevelt suggested that a goal *is the execution of a dream*. That is a great definition. Another way of saying it might be that a goal is a dream turned into achievable chunks of reality.

As an example, many professional coaches have had a dream of winning an NFL championship. This resulted in the goal of winning their division. There was an even smaller goal of winning a certain number of games, which was then subdivided into winning several particular games. This resulted from goals of making touchdowns and extra points. That goal was reduced to making a series of first downs and ultimately the necessity of gaining two or three yards on a particular play. These similar goals were articulated by the defensive unit as well. And if you study the sport, you will find that players have individual goals of their own during each game.

All achievements in life are the same. For a goal to be achieved you must have a stated objective. For whatever reason, it seems more effective when the objective is written. This is followed by a specific plan with a target date attached. The objective and the plan must agree with your values. The objective needs to be measurable with a reward for achievement. You need to know what the payoff is. Each of these factors also needs to be written. Learn to set goals today. It will speed you along the road to success. Remember, before the Green Bay Packers were world champions, winning a game was a goal. Before Coach Lombardi was an NFL coach, coaching the pros was the goal. Before you can experience success it must be a goal. Set goals today. Make them specific and make certain they're yours. Then baby step toward turning your dream into a reality.

———————————

*If you don't know where you're going, how do you expect to get there?*

—Basil S. Walsh

## Goals

I once consulted with a very successful young businessman in a personal coaching relationship. He had begun experiencing less success in his career after being promoted into a new position. This new position required him to travel a great deal. Though he was imminently qualified and was deserving of the promotion, he appeared to sabotage this opportunity. Early in the session he began lamenting that he didn't feel successful.

As we began to look further into his life, the conflict became clear. His values, goals, and behaviors had been consistent in his previous position. The problems began with the promotion. In his previous position he was not required to travel. He was able to coach both of his children's softball teams and assist with their soccer team. The promotion meant he couldn't coach. It wasn't a lack of success which troubled him. It was responsibilities that conflicted with his values.

He ultimately realized living within his values *was success*. Even though he was performing the responsibilities of his new position, he didn't really value being away from his family. This resulted in failure feelings. After clarifying the conflict he had a difficult decision to make. His resolution was to level with the company president who had tremendous respect for his employee's honesty and values. The president allowed this man to remain in his new position but delegate the travel requirements to someone else who valued the opportunity to travel. It was a win-win situation. Set goals consistent with your values. This way you are far more likely to succeed. Everyone can win. Anything less and you will feel like a failure. Investigate your values. Learn them. Then set goals consistent with what you believe to be important.—JB

---

*In whatever position you find yourself, determine first your objective.*
—**Marshal Ferdinand Foch**

Goals

SETTING and attaining goals is extremely important. It is equally important, however, to enjoy the day-to-day journey including the struggles. The key to peace of mind while achieving goals is to live in the present moment and enjoy both arriving at your destination and the journey itself.

In the Fall of 1996 Nissan began an extremely successful new marketing program. The campaign, interestingly enough, didn't suggest viewers purchase a Nissan. The message repeated a different mantra. *Life is a journey. Enjoy the ride.* The journey to achieving your goals may be a long one. Along with Nissan, we encourage you to enjoy the ride. The fact is, if you ride long enough, you may get a flat tire. You'll run into some detours. You may have to get jump-started occasionally. Unfortunately, if you ride enough, you may have an accident. All of these happen on a journey. Every journey has a goal. It's your destination. The journey of life is no different.

Take the time today to set out a specific program in your success journal. Describe what your goals are. Think about where you want to go in life. Explain in detail the specific plans and methods for achieving your goals. Ensure they are measurable and include a target date. What time do you expect to arrive? Verify that your goals agree with your core values. List a payoff for achieving your goals. Begin following this plan immediately. You cannot be the best without aspiring to the top. Set your goals high, almost out of reach. Shoot high. After a specific amount of time, you can always re-evaluate them if you want to. And, oh yeah. Don't forget to enjoy the ride.

----

*Do your best to present yourself to God as one approved, a workman who does not need to be ashamed and who correctly handles the word of truth.*

—2 Timothy 2:15

# Mission

MISSION (mish´en) n. 1. A self-imposed duty which gives life purpose and worth. 2. Coach Lombardi and the Green Bay Packers had a mission. It read, "Winning isn't everything, it's the only thing." Everything the Packers did was judged against this mission statement. Is what we're doing right now helping us win? Fairly and squarely within the rules, will it help us win? If it does, do it. If not, stop and do something that will help us win.

By now you should be getting a sense of the hierarchy of success. First come the principles you choose to live by. Then comes your mission, consistent with your principles, against which you judge your actions. Then come your long-term and short-term goals. If it's not in writing, you don't have a mission. What you have is a good idea. Good ideas don't last long in the face of stress and adversity. I have two mission statements. One for my overall life and one for that part of my life as a professional speaker. My mission statement as a speaker reads, "To help people understand the process of growth, change and improved performance. To show people how to paint their own picture of excellence and how to move toward that picture on a want to, choose to, like it, love it basis."

Everything I do professionally is judged against this statement. It's short and to the point. It's easy for me to see what I must do to achieve this mission. This mission inspires me. It gives my work meaning. It's easy to keep in mind during the distracting periods of fatigue, tension, and stress. Your mission statement needs to do the same for you. And it needs to be in writing.—VL, Jr.

---

*If you believe in yourself and have the courage, the determination, the dedication, the competitive drive and if you are willing to sacrifice the little things in life and pay the price for the things that are worthwhile, it can be done.*

—Coach Lombardi

## Mission

YOUR personal mission statement guides you to do the right thing instead of the impulsive thing. If you feel you are on a mission it's much easier to stay on course. Without it you're more likely to give in to impulse.

A mission gives your life integrity. It keeps you going in the right direction. Base your mission statement on that which gives your life meaning. With repetition it can become habitual. Eventually your entire life will be guided by your mission statement. If it works for corporations like Dow Chemical, McDonald's, and Mohawk Carpets, it will work for you.

Begin thinking about a mission statement for your life. It may take awhile. Make it consistent with everything you have done up to this point. After several rewritings you will probably arrive at the beginning of a mission statement. If you find it helpful, begin with the words: *My mission is . . .* Most successful people can state their mission in a short paragraph. Remember, your mission may be totally different from your job. Your job may be something you do for a paycheck. Your mission represents everything you value and want to accomplish with your life. *My mission and passion is to help high achievers balance their lives and experience long-term peak performance. You know how textbooks discuss the life cycle of a product? What I specialize in is the life cycle of your success. There are ways to avoid burning out, self-sabotaging, or dying young. You really can achieve professional success, realize individual fulfillment, and live a long, productive life. You just need the right road map.* Join the company of highly successful people and those on the journey. Begin to write your mission statement today.—JB

---

*Whatever your hand finds to do, do it with all your might.*
—Ecclesiastes 9:10a NIV

## Mission

I spent a year and ten months in Vietnam. Many unusual—and at times surreal—experiences occurred during those twenty-two months. One of the most bizarre occurred on a reconnaissance patrol that was actually in the mountains of Laos.

I was a liaison with a group of Korean soldiers accompanied by several Montagnard tribesmen. We were searching for a particular suspected North Vietnamese hospital location. What we found was totally unexpected. During our foray near the Ho Chi Mihn trail we found a hospital. But it was not what we expected. It was a hospital staffed by European and American missionaries. When we first located them I actually thought I was hallucinating. Later I thought they were possibly French people left over from the French colonial days. When I finally located the Americans we began our discussions. It became clear what was going on. They weren't aiding and abetting the enemy. They were there helping people and later helped us on several occasions.

I became close friends with one particular couple who had children living in Chicago. After returning home I located their children and visited with them. The fascinating thing was that both the parents and the children gave the same explanation as to why they remained in Vietnam and Laos. They described it simply in one sentence. *It's our mission.* That's the intensity and commitment you want to feel with your own personal statement. Make it so strong that in the face of adversity, conflict, and even threats on your life, you can choose to remain on course. Once you achieve this attitude toward your mission, nothing can stand in your way. And in fact, you'll convert others! Work on your mission statement today.

---

*Financial success comes second. My greatest accomplishment is raising my children to be caring, contributing members of the world.*
—Caroline Rose Hunt

## Mission

OVER the years I have worked as a consultant or speaker for various successful companies. I don't think it's coincidental that every successful business I've ever been affiliated with has their mission statement prominently displayed in a public area. It's true without exception. Most successful people I know follow a similar ritual. They have a personal mission statement written and posted where it can be referred to regularly. Sometimes it's on a wall in their office. At other times it is recorded in their day planner. Wherever it may be, it's written and referred to regularly.

A personal mission statement is similar to a holy calling for successful people. They are zealous about their mission statement. They believe in it. They tell you about it. Occasionally they literally wear it on their clothing. Begin to think about your mission statement. It will place you in the company of winners.

Remember, your mission statement is your foundation of success. It is a theme which represents everything discussed up to this point. Your mission statement results from deep thought, inquiry, and study. The first draft is never your last. It embodies all you consider important and contains your hope for the future. It may be a brief paragraph or may consist of a few sentences. In your success journal begin working on it today. Be patient. One of my mentors made me spend literally months on my mission statement. It evolved and finally we both were satisfied. The work was worth it. But don't be surprised if it takes awhile.—JB

---

*An unemployed existence is a worse negation of life than death itself. Because to live means to have something definite to do—a mission to fulfill—and in the measure in which we avoid setting our life to something, we make it empty . . . Human life, by its very nature, has to be dedicated to something.*

—Josè Ortega y Gasset

# Planning

PLANNING (plan´ing) n. 1. Detailed schemes, programs, or methods worked out beforehand for the accomplishment of a goal. 2. When Packers' quarterback Bart Starr attended his first meeting with Coach Lombardi he was impressed with the planning and preparation Lombardi brought to the meeting. He was so impressed, that at the first break he rushed to the phone, called his wife and told her, "We're going to win!"

It has been said that Abraham Lincoln once remarked, "Failing to prepare is preparing to fail." This encapsulates a universal truth. I fully subscribe to the belief that clear, vivid, precise goals, reviewed and visualized daily, will draw to you the means whereby you will achieve them. But that's no excuse for not having a detailed plan for how you will achieve your goal. Is your mission worthwhile? Are your goals worthy of you? If they are—or—if so, they deserve plans for making them achievable.

Your mission and goals are your destination. Your plans are the map and compass that help you reach it. Your plans need to be thorough and flexible. Don't suffer paralysis by analysis. Living in Seattle, I hike with family and friends in the Cascade Mountains just east of the city. We start out with a destination in mind but sometimes get sidetracked by a trail that looks inviting. We often end up in a place more beautiful than our original destination. Flexible planning allows such opportunities. Your mission and goals describe *what* you want to achieve. They are like the final score in a game. You don't win a game by looking at the score board. It's the game plan that assures your success. No team enters a contest without a game plan. The game plan and the successful execution of the game plan determine the winner. Planning is a significant baby step to your success.—VL, Jr.

---

*Confidence comes from planning and practicing well. You get ready during the week and the confidence will be there on Sunday. This confidence is a difficult thing to explain. But you do get it if you have prepared.*

—Coach Lombardi

Planning

IN 1991 the world stood on the edge of what many people felt would be the Battle of Armageddon. Scholars, prophets, and charlatans believed the end-of-the-world battle was about to occur. The anti-climactic response was in actuality the result of multiple years of behind-the-scenes planning. The battle began after the air strikes and bombing concluded. The ground war only took a few days. Armageddon was either avoided or robbed of its prophetic glory depending on your perspective. This particular war has been analyzed by many military strategists and will continue to be in the future. All have agreed that the success of the war was a result of planning. The planning was done by two brilliant and successful strategists, General Norman Schwarzkopf and General Colin Powell.

Successful people plan and prepare far more than the average person. In fact their painstaking preparation can be irritating to those less enlightened. Whether these people are in the military, business, sports, the arts, or any other venue, planning is one of the keys to their success. It is also one of the most vital. If you want to succeed, you must plan for success.

Former Green Bay Packer quarterback Bart Starr and many others have commented on the hours of preparation and planning Lombardi would put into his practices and games. Sunday, game day, was always the easiest day of the week. There were often eighteen-hour days, sleeping in the locker room, physical and mental practices that would begin early in the morning and go late into the evening. The result is in the Packers' success. Make no mistake about it. Planning and preparation are synonymous with success.

---

*Thoroughness characterizes all successful men. Genius is the art of taking infinite pains . . . All great achievement has been characterized by extreme care, infinitely painstaking, even to the minutest detail.*
—Elbert Hubbard

## Planning

I am an avid parachutist. Though I haven't jumped in several years, I thoroughly enjoy the sport. Statistically speaking, it is actually quite safe. Far more people die playing golf or watching baseball games than from parachuting. But the threat of danger is constantly there. It's the hours of planning and preparation that make it far less dangerous than it appears.

As a former military parachutist, I disagree with one aspect of sport parachuting. In the military, jump school is a three week program. Civilian jump school takes one day. You literally attend one day of training and make a parachute jump that afternoon. I have attended several of these schools and never witnessed anyone injured in civilian parachuting. Yet I think not enough time goes into *planning*. In military jump school they probably plan to excess. And it's true, military parachuting is far more risky and complex. Let's face it. Rarely is anyone going to shoot at you in civilian parachuting. Likewise there are rarely mass jumps of several hundred people in the air at the same time.

The point remains that planning is an important part of military parachuting. The difference between the civilian one-day jump school and a three-week military parachuting school is not in the requirements of jumping out of the plane. It is in the time spent planning. You plan until your reactions become automatic. That way you avoid confusion and possible injury. Parachuting is not that different from the rest of life. It's filled with equal opportunity for ecstasy and tragedy. Life will give you every possible option. You can soar, crash and burn, or virtually anything in between. The difference is often found in one key word: *planning*. Start today.—JB

---

*Make no little plans; they have no magic to stir men's blood . . . Make big plans; aim high in hope and work, remembering that a noble, logical diagram once recorded will never die.*
—Daniel Hudson Burnham

Planning
--------

WHEN going on a trip, you plan. When organizing your closet or chest of drawers, you plan. And even when you are going to cook a meal, you plan. It may be called a menu, a blueprint, a road map, or some other such description, but it is simply a plan. Somehow though we often fail at planning our lives.

In ancient Rome there was a unique custom that assisted in planning. The great arches of Rome, still standing some 2000 years later, were designed by various architects. The arches were planned to last and they have. Perhaps the reason they still stand is due to the planning. But the reason for the planning is the most interesting. While the scaffolding was being removed from the arch, the architect had to stand underneath it. If the arch fell, he was crushed. As I said—most of the arches are still standing. Planning as if your life depends on it may be the thing to do.

Today take this baby step. Begin to design your plan for success in your journal. Realize that it will take many drafts before it is complete. But begin your planning today. Planning should be as detailed and specific as possible. Spend hours or even days to achieve your comprehensive plan. When you think you are ready to remove "the scaffolding," stand underneath your plan and test it. What does the plan look like? A sample plan will be in the workbook. Plan as if your success depends on it. It does. Even better, plan as if your life depends on it. It probably does, too. Take your time during planning. It may require weeks. Get feedback from friends. Buy a book that discusses business plans and marketing plans. These will begin to help you understand the complexity and significance of this task. People can spend thousands of dollars and hundreds of hours on a business plan. Your life is at least as important as a business plan. It will give you confidence to stand under the arches as the scaffolding is removed. Are you ready?

---

*For whatsoever a man soweth, that shall he also reap.*
                                                    —Galatians 6:7b

# Contingency Planning

CONTINGENCY PLANNING (kon-tin´jen-se plan´ing) v. 1. To formulate a detailed or alternative program or strategy for an event or possibility that may occur. A contingency plan is put in place in the event the primary strategy fails. 2. Coach Lombardi demonstrated this principle by always having a back-up play in case one failed. Better than that, he practiced these emergency plays as hard as the others. He insisted that his players know each one well enough to execute it without thinking.

Contingency plans are as important as primary goals as long as they don't diffuse your focus. I have four adult children. As they grew up I advised them to develop options in their lives. My suggestions included getting advanced degrees to widen their possibilities. But my advice was intended to expand their options not necessarily to change or diffuse their focus. Everyone needs a contingency plan. But it doesn't have to detract from your primary goal.

The example I gave in the planning chapter applies here as well. I related how we stay open-minded in our treks through the mountains. If we see a better path we take it. Our real goal is to enjoy the scenery and fresh air. No matter which path we take the goal remains the same. The goal is not to reach a certain point in the mountains. It is to spend time together and enjoy the outdoors. Some people get confused as to what their true goals are. Thinking about contingency plans can help you clarify your goals. They don't change the destination. They provide an alternate plan for reaching it. Have a back-up plan. Remain open-minded. But make sure it's not a diversion.—VL, Jr.

---

*Fundamentals win it. Football is two things: it's blocking and it's tackling. I don't care anything about formation or new offenses or tricks on defense. If you block and tackle better than the team you're playing, you'll win.*

—Coach Lombardi

## Contingency Planning

IN a previous chapter I discussed parachuting. I have jumped out of perfectly good airplanes over three hundred times. I was in charge of parachuting at Camp Pendleton Marine Corps Base many years ago. I have great respect for the sport and even greater respect for the danger involved. Though I realize parachuting is usually safe, I believe in taking precautions. One of those precautions is to have a reserve parachute. If the main canopy is defective or doesn't open I want a reserve. I have never used my reserve. But I want it, just in case.

One part of any good plan is having a reserve. When it comes to a life plan your reserve parachute is the back-up plan. It is your alternative when the primary plan doesn't work. Having a contingency plan isn't predicting disaster. Having a spare tire in your trunk doesn't mean you're going to have a flat. Just because you back up material on your computer doesn't mean you think the system is going to fail. When you go out on a small boat, the laws in most states require a life jacket. Cruise ships carry life boats. These are contingency plans.

If you plan well, you will always have a reserve. Focus on your main plan. Pursue it passionately. If for some reason it doesn't work, go to your contingency plan. Your back-up plan will not usually take you in a totally different direction. A reserve parachute is still a parachute. It may be smaller or have a slightly different shape. However it still returns you to earth. You go in the same direction—down! It's the same with any contingency plan. Your destination may remain identical, but the means of arrival might change slightly. Have an alternate course of action. It will help you on the journey to success.—JB

---

*The sluggard will not plow by reason of the cold; therefore shall he beg in harvest, and have nothing.*

—Proverbs 20:4

## Contingency Planning

SEVERAL years ago I was showing one of my sons some pictures taken when I was a young man in Vietnam. At the time of this conversation he was ten years old and very inquisitive about the photographs. One of the questions he asked was why we were wearing scarves. I looked at the particular picture he was referring to and noticed that each of the people in the photo did have a "scarf" somewhere on his body. I had one around my neck, used another as a belt, and improvised a third as a sling for my AK-47 rifle. Other people had them tied around their foreheads and draped in other places.

I told him they weren't actually scarves. I explained that they were bandannas and were intended to be medical wrappings. In Vietnam we were accustomed to using them for various diverse purposes. They could certainly be used for medical reasons. I used them more than once to stop bleeding or mend wounds. They were also very useful for tying braces and splints. You could use them to bathe with or as a towel. A friend of mine even used his once as wrapping paper for children's gifts. I used my bandanna because of its versatility. It was a "contingency rag."

In many ways the bandanna was like a reserve parachute. It was a contingency plan. It was there as a backup for a variety of items that were not available. It worked in Vietnam and *the concept* has worked virtually the rest of my life. Perhaps you need a similar contingency rag in your life. Today, I carry a pen that has four fillers. I have another pen in my wallet and also one in my day planner. I have a micro-cassette recorder in my pocket and on my bedside. I also have a voice pager/organizer that has memo-recording capability. I'm a speaker and writer. Pens and recorders are my tools. I have back-ups! So should you.—JB

---

*Divide your movement into easy-to-do sections. If you fail, divide again.*

—Peter Nivio Zarlenga

Contingency Planning

IN the 1981 NFL championship game the Forty-Niners were trailing Tom Landry's Cowboys. It was the fourth quarter and maestro Joe Montana was driving down the field. Fans had seen it before. Montana, along with Bart Starr and more recently John Elway, was known for leading his team down the field in fourth quarter drives. This particular series of plays looked rather hopeless. The Niner line was simply not able to keep the defense of the Cowboys from troubling Montana. What they had not counted on was the Niner's contingency plan. Coach Bill Walsh was packing a reserve parachute.

On what appeared to be the last play of the drive, Montana was aggressively rushed by the Cowboy's defense. He scrambled out of the pocket. It appeared to be a broken play but had in fact been practiced hundreds of times as a reserve. If the Niner's receiver corps saw Montana scrambling, they were trained to go to certain points on the field and try to break open. Knowing this, Montana threw the ball to a spot without even seeing his receiver. Six-foot-five inch Dwight Clark waited at that spot. He leapt above the defender in the back of the end zone and caught the winning pass. The Forty-niners won the game as a result of that play.

This play was a perfect example of having a contingency plan. It wasn't a miracle. It was a well thought out and practiced back-up plan. When things aren't going right have a fail-safe mechanism. Take this baby step today. Begin to expand the plan in your journal to include an emergency plan of action. Make it something that is not your primary plan. It's only there *in case your main parachute doesn't open.* By doing so you will experience greater confidence on the road to success.

---

*Developing the plan is actually laying out the sequence of events that have to occur for you to achieve your goal.*
—George L. Morrisey

# Beginning
# to
# Think for Success

*There is no success without hardship.*

—Sophocles

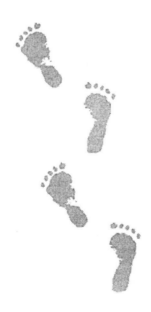

# Focus

FOCUS (fo´cus) n. 1. The center of your interest or activity, also referred to as singleness of purpose. 2. Coach Lombardi had that rare ability to focus on something to the exclusion of everything else around him. Driving down the highway, focusing on what play to run on third and long, he'd miss his exit. As a young high school coach living with his family in one of those post World War II housing tracts, he had a particular problem. All the houses looked alike. Lombardi often would come home at night, concentrating on a problem. He would park the car, walk into the kitchen, and discover he was in the wrong house.

The question is, how did Coach Lombardi achieve the success he did? Each of the fifty-two qualities laid out in this book is the broad answer. But the ability to focus, to bring a white-hot concentration to the business at hand, would have to rank at the top. People say Vince Lombardi would have been a success at anything. He could have been a great lawyer or a successful CEO of a Fortune 500 company. That's probably true, but it's doubtful he would have achieved the same success as he did as a football coach. *Football was his medium. Rembrandt had his oils, Coach Lombardi had football.*

How fortunate are those few people, like Coach Lombardi, who feel so strongly about a goal that they are able to muster every fiber of their being to focus on achieving it. If there is a purpose in your life that you feel as zealous about as he did about football, you are blessed. The rest of us will need to keep searching. If you're like many people, you're still looking for that all-consuming purpose. You're looking for your *medium.* In the meantime, you have no excuse not to muster as much focus as possible, for whatever is before you at this moment.—VL, Jr.

---

*Success demands singleness of purpose.*

—Coach Lombardi

## Focus

". . . I do one thing. I do it very well. And then I move on . . ."
Charles Emerson Winchester III was one of the characters in the
award-winning TV series M.A.S.H. In this particular episode he was
responding to some harassment by his fellow surgeons. They didn't
think he was moving quickly enough. That is an example of focus.
Choose one thing. Become an expert at it. Feel passionate about it.
And then do it well. Charles Emerson Winchester III may not have
been popular, but even in the series his competency was never questioned.

To achieve that kind of focus, it's extremely important to love
what you do, and do what you love. To be focused, you need to be
passionate about your focus, regardless of what it is. It's fascinating
to visit different countries. In Japan people make an art form out of
tending their gardens, having tea ceremonies, or studying martial
arts. They take the object of their passion and turn it into an
obsession of sorts. The Japanese tea ceremony can take hours. A
traditional Japanese martial art becomes a lifestyle. A beautiful
Japanese garden takes a lifetime of work. Take whatever you do and
turn it into something about which you can become passionate.
This will make it far easier for you to focus.

Coach Lombardi said that success demands singleness of purpose.
This is an intense focus which eliminates distractions. Singleness
of purpose means doing one thing but doing it well. Focus and you
will succeed. Emulate Charles Emerson Winchester III. Do one
thing. Do it well. And then move on.

---

*The weakest living creature, by concentrating his powers on a single
object, can accomplish something; whereas the strongest, by dispersing
his over many, may fail to accomplish anything.*
                                                    —Thomas Carlyle

## Focus

IN the movie *City Slickers*, Jack Palance played the memorable character of "Curly." In a discussion with Billy Crystal, Curly held up one finger and explained to Crystal it was the secret to happiness. Crystal asked if Curly meant his *finger* was the secret to happiness. Palance said, "No, it's one thing." Crystal asked the next logical question, "What is that one thing?" Palance smiled and said, "That's what you have to find out."

The secret to *happiness* in all likelihood may be several things. However, the secret to *success* is Curly's secret. If you truly want to be successful, you need to focus on one thing. The writers of the movie *City Slickers* were correct. It's your job—and a tough job—to discover what that one thing is. There are probably a number of areas in which you could excel. Sifting through them and isolating "one thing" is a painful but necessary process. I recently had a version of this conversation with a friend who is a surgeon. He was beginning to develop a specialized limited practice, but was having tremendous anxiety about it. All the studies and statistics indicated it was a wise move, but insecurity prevented him from following through. It's difficult to quit being a generalist, but Curly's secret "one thing" apparently is correct.

I have heard different people say similar things. Some say, "Find something you would do for free and do it. Money will follow." Thoreau suggested, "Live the life *you* have imagined." The advice of philosophers and other brilliant people is the same. Choose one thing. Focus on it. You will succeed. This one is tough. In reality you probably can do many things well. That's not the point. Mastery requires focus. "Doing many things well" is different than mastery. On the path to success mastery is a vital tool. And mastery is gained through focus.

---

*The soul that has no established aim loses itself.*
—**Michel de Montaigne**

## Focus

THE neurological reality is that your mind cannot focus on two contrasting thoughts simultaneously. It *focuses* on thoughts very rapidly. But it can only focus on one at a time. As a result it is easy to be disrupted by distractions. This is true for you as a person. It's also true for corporate America. Author Al Ries discusses this topic in detail in his classic book, *Focus*. He suggests that the quality major companies possess is their ability to focus.

The key is to focus on one goal at a time. Conceptualize the goal in your mind. Convince yourself you can achieve it. And then pursue it. Focus is seeing the goal that you want to achieve and allowing that picture to drive you forward. You can't focus on two dissimilar thoughts simultaneously. Choose only one and make it an intense focus. Take this baby step today. In your journal write a completely honest paragraph or page on each of the following questions. What do you enjoy doing so much that you would do it for free? If you could be the world's leading expert on one specific area or topic, what would it be? Assume for a fact you have sixty days of perfect health to live. At the end of these sixty days you will die a peaceful death. What will you fill your time with in those last sixty days? The last six days? The last sixty minutes? What do you enjoy doing to the degree that it *gives* you energy? What do you enjoy doing so much that you lose track of time while involved in it?

After answering these questions develop a primary goal for the next three months. Make it your "one thing" for the next quarter. Think about it. Obsess over it. Desire it. Bury yourself in it. Love it. Focus on it. Do it for three months. Focus. And you will succeed.

---

*Blessed are they that keep his testimonies, and that seek him with the whole heart.*

—Psalm 119:2

# Reality Orientation

REALITY ORIENTATION (re-al´e-te or´e-en-ta´shen) n. 1. The state of being actual or true. 2. Coach Lombardi understood that if his staff and team didn't deal in reality they would fail. Each Monday would begin with an honest assessment of his own coaching the previous day. If they lost, he willingly took responsibility. Then came a critique of each player's effort. Finally, Lombardi and his staff began a realistic appraisal of the next team they were scheduled to play. To prepare a winning game plan, they needed a realistic understanding of the strengths and weaknesses of next Sunday's opponent.

Most people want to grow and change. Yet growth is often painfully slow in coming. For some, the problem is that they never look at current reality. Goals in the future are important. But it's just as important that you be honest about your current situation. If you delude yourself you lose the discomfort that can be converted into motivation. I have a goal to weigh 170 pounds. I can't seem to get there. 180 pounds is about the best that I can do. My goal of 170 pounds is very clear, vivid, and precise. I know what it will look like when I get on the scale and see the needle go to 170. I know how my clothes will feel when I weigh 170. I know what it will sound like when people say to me, "Vince, you're looking good, did you loose a little weight?"

Why can't I lose the weight? Because I don't look at current reality. I never get on the scale. All I do is stand in front of the mirror, and say, "Pretty good. Not bad for a man of my age." There's no discomfort that I can convert into motivation I need to lose weight. I've got to check current reality every day. And reality is on the scale, not in my mirror. When I see 180 pounds on the scale every day, sufficient discomfort will be created. I'll be motivated to do things to reach my goal. Ken Blanchard, co-author of the *One Minute Manager* says, "Feedback is the breakfast of champions." He is correct. Feedback ". . . where I am (reality) in relation to where I want to go (my goals) . . . is the breakfast of champions."—VL, Jr.

---

*A leader must be honest with himself and know that as a leader he is just like everybody else.*

—Coach Lombardi

## Reality Orientation

LEARNING to see things as they really are is gaining consciousness. You learn it the same way you learned to ride a bicycle. At some point in life, probably as a child, you couldn't ride a bicycle and were perfectly satisfied not knowing about it. You were oblivious and unaware, and it was fine. You were *unconsciously incompetent*.

Later you saw someone whiz by on a ten-speed. At that moment you became *consciously incompetent*. With conscious incompetence you had awareness. Awareness brought discomfort. That discomfort brought an accompanying degree of pain which could only be alleviated by learning to ride a bicycle. Afterwards an incredible learning curve occurred. You practiced. You skinned your elbows and hurt your knees. Consciousness brought with it responsibility and responsibility brought pain. But before long you could ride the bike. You pedaled. You balanced. You steered. You became more coordinated and concentrated on enjoying it. But that was the problem. You still had to think. You were *consciously competent*. It required special energy to concentrate and left you somewhat awkward.

You continued to ride your bike. You practiced the art for hours, days, and even years. Before long you no longer had to think about it. You got on the bicycle and became one with it. It was an extension of your body. Concentration was no longer required. You achieved *unconscious competence*—a sign of mastery. You were poetry in motion. Your awareness no longer required you to think consciously. Whether learning to ride a bike, play an instrument, or master a baby step, this is the journey of consciousness. It takes awhile, but you experience incredible freedom once you've mastered it. You can become unconsciously competent with success. And when you do, you'll be liberated.

---

*Humankind cannot bear very much reality.*

—T. S. Eliot

## Reality Orientation

MANY years ago Tom, a race-car driver, called me for a consultation. He had been involved in a serious racing accident and was having nightmares about it. He was going around a blind curve and for some reason had begun slowing down to an unusually slow pace. A number of other cars sped past him and ran into a pile-up. Several people were injured and a few were hurt quite seriously. Tom skirted onto the infield of the raceway, passed the pile-up, and won the race. However the victory was a hollow one.

Tom was having tremendous anxiety wondering why he slowed down. He felt guilty about winning the race. It didn't make sense to him that he slowed down and everyone else didn't. The nightmares that followed haunted him. We discussed his dreams and I made some suggestions on how to learn from them. Shortly after our third session he phoned and explained what had occurred. This time his nightmare had been in slow motion. As Tom neared the curve he noticed the grandstands in his peripheral vision. As the slow motion panorama continued he noticed that instead of looking at him, the fans were staring ahead beyond the blind curve. Several were pointing. Others had looks of horror on their faces. A few covered their eyes as if they didn't want to see what was happening. At the same time he saw himself applying the brakes, gearing down, and slowing his rate of speed. He saw it all in slow motion.

He began to realize his reaction was a result of unconscious competence. He actually saw the dangerous reality of the situation without even being aware. His questions concerning why he slowed down were answered. If you open your eyes, the same thing will happen to you. You will begin to see things as they really are. You'll begin to notice. You'll begin to realize. And what you'll see is usually not what you thought you would. Most people don't live a full life because they're deluded. They are blinded by their fears and shadows of reality. Wake up. See things as they really are. It will speed you along as you baby step toward success.—JB

---

*And you shall know the truth, and the truth shall make you free.*
—John 8:32

Reality Orientation

TOO many people spend their time in self-delusion. They see things not as they really are but as they want them to be. Others see things as they feel they *should be*. Only a few see things as they really are. Most people are blinded by their emotions. Some blame other people for their misperception.

Our opinion is that self-deception and self-delusion are the only kind of misperceptions. Certainly, others can give us the wrong information. But it's your own emotion—usually fear—that keeps you from seeing things as they really are. The 1995 movie *Crimson Tide* gave a good example of how self-delusion on a small scale could change the course of world events. It was both a powerful and believable rendition. A real-life example of self-deception occurred in July 1990 when an Air Florida 737 flight crashed into the Potomac killing seventy-eight people. From transcripts of conversations between the pilot and copilot, it's obvious that a tremendous amount of self-deception occurred.

Stop deluding yourself. Take off your rose-colored glasses and see things as they really are. Forget how you want them to be, or how your parents said they should be. Don't make the mistake of imagining what you want reality to be and then reacting to it—good or bad. Take this baby step today. In your success journal make a list of at least ten ways you have deceived yourself in the past two years. Then make plans to correct these misperceptions.

---

*Reality isn't the way you wish things to be, nor the way they appear to be, but the way they actually are.*
                                                    —Robert J. Ringer

# Commitment

COMMITMENT (ka-mit´ment) n. 1. The state of being bound emotionally or intellectually to some course of action; that quality that's necessary before real change can occur. 2. Coach Lombardi's sense of commitment was legendary. His players saw that he worked harder and longer than they did. Because Lombardi was so clearly committed, he could demand total commitment from his players. Those who could not, or would not, approach his level of commitment, were soon playing for another team.

Coach Lombardi is widely quoted as saying, "The quality of a person's life is in direct proportion to their commitment to excellence." What precisely is this commitment that can define the quality of your life? When you commit to a goal, you make a firm, strong decision to do something. The Latin root for decision is to "cut away from" as in an incision. So when you commit, what you're really doing is cutting away all other options. When you commit, you cut away all the excuses.

Cus D'Amato managed and trained fighters. He adopted and raised Mike Tyson. It was only after D'Amato passed away that Tyson began to experience his problems. A writer once asked D'Amato if one of his fighters was ready for a bout. "About 90%," replied the manager. The writer remarked that the fighter had been training for months and wanted to know why he wasn't ready. Cus D'Amato said a fighter never gets in the ring thinking he is 100%. If he did and lost, he might never fight again. Most people have a tendency to do that. Most go after their goals with about 90% commitment. That leaves 10% to make an excuse with. Commitment is 100% effort, 100% of the time. Here's the kicker. If you can't see it, you can't commit to it. Unless your goals are clear, vivid, and precise, you can't enlist the awesome power of commitment. Can you see, taste, touch, hear and smell it? If the answer is yes, then your are ready to commit to your goal.—VL, Jr.

---

*If you fellows don't want to give me a hundred percent, get on up to the club house and turn in your equipment.*
—Coach Lombardi

Commitment
----------

IN 1541 Hernando Cortes invaded the Mayans in southwest Mexico. He brought eleven ships with him in the invasion. He rallied his troops and apparently gave a rousing speech. As they climbed the mountains toward the Mayan villages, the soldiers looked back and saw smoke from the beach. Cortes had instructed the few men remaining on the beach to burn the ships. It was his way of ensuring his troops' commitment to the battle. "We are either going to die together or win the struggle and go home. But there is no turning back without victory."

In order to be great at anything, you must be totally committed. This means reducing the possibility of turning back. When Cortes burned the ships, he was making a fascinating symbolic and literal statement. The soldiers were apparently convinced. They eventually won the battle. In circumstances where you make 100% commitment there is more sense of resolve. Distractions and fantasies become less of a bother. Once you're as committed as Cortes, there is no wavering, or turning back. You can only go forward. Success, at this point, is only a matter of time.

This kind of commitment, combined with focus, can ensure success in virtually any endeavor. Rally your troops. Give them a rousing speech. Then begin to do as Cortes did. Lead from the front. Make a commitment. Burn your ships. Then take one baby step at a time toward the mountains. Prepare yourself for a struggle. One certainly awaits you. Success is not easy. If it was, everyone would already have it. For most people the journey is a long one. There are a few for whom it seems brief. Tiger Woods won the Masters Golf tournament at age twenty-one. He was the youngest ever to win. He was also the first Asian or Black American to win. And he won with the best score in history. And he's only twenty-one! Couldn't have played a lot of golf and be just twenty-one, huh? Wrong! He began playing at age three. It was a long journey for Tiger as well. But his commitment paid off. Yours can too—*one baby step at a time.*

---

**Commit everything you do to the Lord. Trust Him to help you do it and he will.**

—Psalm 37:5 LB

## Commitment

AFTER a keynote speech a participant asked me a question which unexpectedly led to a discussion about commitment. The participant requested me to comment on why I thought Asian immigrants were so successful in American schools and business. After a few minutes of discussion the suggestion was made that perhaps it's because of their level of commitment. "They burn their ships." I suggested. For many of them, it's either succeed or starve. There's no turning back. Several weeks later I received a note in the mail from her with the following quote from Goethe.

" . . . Until one is committed there is hesitancy, a chance to draw back . . . There is one elementary truth, the ignorance of which kills countless ideas and splendid plans. That is, that the moment one definitely commits oneself then providence moves too. All sorts of things occur to help one that would never otherwise have occurred. A whole stream of events issues from the decision raising in one's favor all manner of unforeseen incidents and material assistance which no man could have dreamt would come his way. Whatever you can do, or dream you can, begin it. Boldness has genius, power and magic in it. Begin it now . . ."

Goethe was a German author, lawyer, and scientist. He is generally recognized as one of the greatest and most versatile writers of modern time. To him poetry and science were all one. He made major contributions to poetry, biology, sociology, morphology, literature, music, art and philosophy. Goethe was immensely qualified to discuss commitment. His commitment was to knowledge.

---

*Men must have goals which, in their eyes, merit effort and commitment; and they must believe that their efforts will win them the respect of others.*

—John W. Garner

## Commitment

COMMITMENT is the critical element in determining long-term success. In reality, it is the critical element in many different factors. No relationship will succeed until each person is committed. There will be no physical health until you are committed to achieving it. Similarly, the same requirement is necessary for your success. Virtually nothing will be accomplished until you are 100% committed to that achievement.

It is easy to write about commitment, but living it is the true test. This is what makes the difference between someone who knows superficially and one who truly succeeds. How committed are you to your own success? Begin to think seriously about that question. Talk to several friends about it. Investigate your own hesitancies and tendencies toward self-sabotage. Pray and meditate about it. Write more in your journal. Begin to review your vision, your plan, and your goals. Renew your focus and commitment.

The biggest obstacle is in the daily struggles you will face. You will be discouraged. Change won't occur as rapidly as you like. People will not be nice to you. You won't be appreciated for your efforts until you don't need their appreciation. You will want to give up and go back to the ships. Full commitment burns the ships and pushes you to reach your full potential. Memorize Goethe! Then take this baby step today. Write yourself a letter and explain which ships you are burning. Make your commitment complete. Give yourself the Cortes solution. There is one way to go home. And that's to win the struggle. Do this and you will be swept along to success.

---

*To fight out a war, you must believe something and want something with all your might. So must you do to carry anything else to an end worth reaching. More than that, you must be willing to commit yourself to a course, perhaps a long and hard one, without being able to foresee exactly where you will come out.*
                                          —**Oliver Wendell Holmes, Jr.**

# Sacrifice

SACRIFICE (sak´ra-fis) n. 1. The forfeiture of something highly valued, for the sake of something considered to have a greater value. 2. Coach Lombardi constantly demanded sacrifice and self-denial from his players. He understood that football is a harsh, brutal sport. The demands the game makes on players and coaches are unlike anything other than warfare. He also made sure the team understood that having made the sacrifice to win, the joy of victory was all the sweeter.

If I had to boil down to a sentence or phrase what my father stood for, it would be, "To accomplish anything worthwhile, you must pay the price." Success takes sacrifice. Success involves making choices and choice means sacrifice. By virtue of the fact that you choose something, something else must be given up. If you determine to get to work an hour earlier, something else must be given up. You either sacrifice an extra hour of sleep or go to bed an hour earlier and forgo watching your favorite TV show.

Success is not a matter of luck or getting a break. It's not a matter of timing or being in the right place at the right time, though these things help. Success follows the law of physics—cause and effect. And the laws of nature—you reap what you sow. There are no short-cuts. There is a price to be paid for success, and that price is sacrifice. There's an often-used saying usually associated with exercise, "No pain, no gain." This phrase has a wider application. Success requires you to endure pain. The pain may not be physical. It could be in giving things up to achieve your success. The pain is in sacrifice. The reward for your pain is success.—VL, Jr.

---

*To achieve success, whatever the job we have, we must pay a price for success. It's like anything worthwhile. It has a price. You have to pay the price to win and you have to pay the price to get to the point where success is possible. Most important, you must pay the price to stay there.*

—Coach Lombardi

Sacrifice

MANY years ago I gave a lady the following advice. "You can't have a $50,000 car and a $50,000 marriage." To put it into context, this particular woman wanted everything. She wanted her husband to meet all her social and emotional needs. She also wanted him to earn the kind of money that could support her "$50,000 car" lifestyle. She also expected him to read her mind. My response was one way of telling her she couldn't have everything. I was speaking figuratively at the time. But there is some degree of truth in my comments.

In reality I do know people who have "$50,000 cars and $50,000 marriages." However I only know a few. In all cases they made enormous sacrifices in their lives. My message is not about cars or marriage. It's about sacrifice. The sacrifice required to succeed at one particular goal will automatically lower the possibility of achieving others. Generally speaking, you must sacrifice somewhere.

To achieve success there is always a price. Sometimes it is another goal, in other instances, people may suffer. Certainly your opportunities for leisure time will suffer. Sacrifice is inevitable and necessary. Success can be yours. You won't succeed at everything you try. In fact, if you try succeeding at everything you will fail at life. Choose your goals well. Delineate them well. And make the necessary sacrifice to succeed. If you do this, success will be yours. Avoid the temptation to cheat. Success cannot be borrowed or purchased on credit. It's earned by the sweat of your brow, one baby step at a time. It requires sacrifice.—JB

---

*There is no victory at bargain basement prices.*
—Dwight D. Eisenhower

## Sacrifice

I grew up in the 1950's in the rural Piedmont section of North Carolina. For most of my childhood I lived with my grandparents. They were extremely good-hearted *country* folks. We lived on a farm and everybody pitched in when it was time to work. Even though *gender equity* was not even a concept in that era, teamwork also applied in the kitchen.

When we wanted fried chicken for supper, there was a particular sacrifice that had to be made. Someone had to enter the hen house and convince one of the chickens to sacrifice her life for our supper. This was a sight to behold. It was by no means pretty. Yet it didn't deter our appetites. Everyone participated. We chased the hen. We convinced her to give her life for our appetite. Then we plucked her, cleaned her, and otherwise prepared our own early version of the "Colonel's choice."

Throughout my life I have learned a great deal from such experiences. (Not only was it a sacrifice on the hen's part, it was a sacrifice for each of us as well.) Everyone worked. Supper did not begin at 7:00 p.m. by picking up the phone and dialing for Dominos. It began in the afternoon, not by going to the grocery store, but by going to our garden and the hen house. If we wanted to eat at six, the sacrifice began around 3:30. "You can play later. We got to get ready for supper now." My grandmother constantly reminded me of the importance of sacrifice. It is an extremely important component on the road to success. The honest truth is difficult to admit. The times that I have not experienced success, and there were many, share one glaring factor in common. It's the times I ignored Grandmother's advice.—JB

---

*Do not love sleep or you will grow poor; stay awake and you will have food to spare.*

**—Proverbs 20:13** NIV

Sacrifice

DELAYED gratification is an important concept to learn. The basic idea is that if you want a greater reward in the long run, you need to delay gratification in the short term. Greater rewards later require short-term sacrifice now. This is the general concept of delayed gratification. It is actually a commentary about the importance of sacrifice.

Most people want success. Few are willing to make the sacrifice. Yet that is the missing ingredient in most people's attempts at winning. A common mantra during Marine Corps training is to, "Sweat in training so you don't bleed in battle." Make the sacrifice now so you succeed later. Personal success in the Marines meant living through each day. That was highly motivating. The payoff for making the sacrifice was to continue living and breathing. What a deal!

What is the payoff for your sacrifice? You need to ask yourself that question and answer it adequately. Most people won't sacrifice if the payoff is insufficient. Perhaps you need to increase or change it. Take this baby step today. Look very closely at the plans you have made thus far. These can be plans you've made in the past, or plans you have made while reading this book. Choose one primary goal. In your success journal list the sacrifices you'll need to make in order to achieve that goal. Next record a corresponding payoff for each. Then begin making them. You will be well on your path to success. Remember, for the Packers, the payoff was a world championship. It needs to be a major payoff for you as well. Make your reward world championship caliber, and you'll achieve world championship success.

---

*There is no royal road; you've got to work a good deal harder than most people want to work.*
—Charles E. Wilson

5

# Doing the Work
# of
# Success

*Success is relative: It is what we can make of the mess we have made of things.*

—T.S. Elliot

# Mental Toughness

MENTAL TOUGHNESS (men´tal tuf´ness) n. 1. The conditioning of the mind which enables one to continue; to keep on fighting despite the presence of doubt, stress, or criticism from others. 2. Coach Lombardi learned mental toughness at an early age. As a college football player at Fordham, he once played an entire game with a cut inside his mouth that later required thirty stitches to close. As a coach he schooled his players in the mental aspects of football. He told them that in order to win, they would need to disregard the minor hurts, ignore the pain, and scorn the pressure applied by opponents and supporters alike.

Mental toughness is the ability to focus on your goal, in the face of adversity. It's holding on to what "you want" in the face of what "you've got." You don't have to be a hulking linebacker to possess mental toughness. Kerri Strug awed us in the 1996 Olympic Games. The sheer determination of her final vault, which produced a 9.712 score despite a badly sprained ankle, has become a part of Olympic lore. She held on to her goal in the face of her current reality of pain, pressure, and competition! Mental toughness came in a four-foot-nine-inch, eighty-seven pound gymnast.

Mental toughness is the willingness, day in and day out, to keep the commitments you make to yourself. It is the willingness, every day, to do the little things that separate the successful people in your chosen profession from everyone else. Mental toughness is not something you're born with. It's learned. You start small, achieving a minor goal. Each time you take on a bigger challenge. You don't win every time, but each challenge is only slightly bigger than before, so it's easy to take a hit and bounce back. Over time your confidence grows until the mental toughness that all successful people possess becomes part of your makeup. —VL, Jr.

---

*Mental toughness is many things and rather difficult to explain. Its qualities are sacrifice and self-denial. Also, most importantly, it is combined with a perfectly disciplined will that refuses to give in. It's a state of mind—you could call it character in action.*

—Coach Lombardi

## Mental Toughness

EVERYONE knows what it means to "get in shape." You buy exercise equipment, join health clubs, and take other measures to strengthen your muscles and build your endurance. It helps your body become physically tough. Few people, however, do what is required to become mentally tough. To succeed over the long term, you need to be mentally as well as physically fit.

Mental toughness is the art of conditioning your character. It means getting your attitude, morale, and spirit in "shape." It means being able to concentrate in the face of distractions and succeed in spite of adversity. It's not being harsh, critical, or negative. In fact, those characteristics are often a sign of mental weakness.

The idea that you must exercise to be in good *physical* condition is readily accepted today. To get in "shape" you have to work at it. Over time you can become physically tough. You are not born physically fit. An infant is truly helpless. But if you work at it, you can gain a high degree of physical fitness. In the same way you are not born mentally fit. It takes time, commitment, and energy. With discipline, mental toughness is within your grasp. If you're a homemaker, mental toughness will help you hang in there even though others don't seem to appreciate your efforts. As an athlete, it will help you when your team is behind and you want to quit. As a sales rep or manager, it will help you in your quest for the top. Practice mental toughness skills and you will be taking a baby step to success. Like the other baby steps you will have difficulty with this one at first. Don't get discouraged. Frankly, few people grow up with this trait. You either learned it through experience and training, or you didn't. It's not genetic. The good news is, regardless of your circumstances, you can begin learning it now.

---

*Never, never, never, never give up.*

—Winston Churchill

## Mental Toughness

IN Vietnam I was shot on two separate occasions. I experienced fear on a daily basis the entire twenty-two months I spent there. More frightening than anything I ever experienced in Vietnam, however, were the drill instructors (DI's) I faced in Marine boot camp and Officer's Candidate School! I was scared to death of my DI's, yet I also had incredible respect for them. They are probably responsible for me being alive today. Were it not for them, I believe I would have been killed instead of merely wounded in combat. I certainly wouldn't be writing this book.

The Marine Corps is where I was first exposed to mental toughness training. I realized the necessity of it, but didn't understand it could mean the difference between life and death. The DI's philosophy seemed to be that if someone wasn't going to break in boot camp they wouldn't break in combat. I believe their theory was sound and it saved hundreds of lives. As an example, if you decided to attempt to run a road race without any prior training, you wouldn't succeed. If you tried to do a hundred push-ups without building up to it, you would fail. Yet over time you can adapt and achieve both of these goals quite easily. Mental toughness is the same way. You have to "work out" to get in shape.

You can learn to adapt to almost any pressure. A mentally tough person can face incredible adversity. Returning POW's, survivors of concentration camps, and torture victims have proven this. Dissect the Lombardi formula for mental toughness. Begin to practice it today. Over time you will become mentally tough. But only with practice. Work at it!—JB

---

*If someone forces you to go with him one mile, go with him two miles.*
—**Matthew 5:41** NIV

## Mental Toughness

YOU *can* overcome adversity. When you're mentally tough you can face any challenge. Since your mind has control over your body, you can direct all your resources toward success. For example, the strong-bodied person who possesses a weak mind will give up easily. However, a strong-minded person, even with a weak body, can still be a high achiever. Yet mental toughness is often ignored. But it wasn't ignored by Coach Lombardi. By breaking mental toughness into Lombardi's definition—*simplicity, spartanism, love for each other, and the perfectly-disciplined will*—you can practice it more readily.

*Simplicity* was a classical Lombardi concept. He liked to focus on a simple plan and a niched goal that could be polished and practiced. Over time it stopped being "practice." It became habit. With enough repetition, it became a way of life. Lombardi's spartanism was the willingness to work with whatever was on hand. (The Spartans were a passionate, heroic people who took what was available and made the most of it. They didn't require a lot of luxuries). By *love for each other*, Lombardi meant charity, humility and contributing to the team rather than focusing only on yourself. He abhorred criticism and pettiness. The *perfectly-disciplined will* was that which realized success could be gained only by hard work. Success is earned by doing what is necessary, even when you don't want to.

Take this baby step today. In your success journal give yourself grades on each of Lombardi's characteristics for mental toughness—*sacrifice, self-denial, humility, charity, dedication, fearlessness, loyalty, simplicity, and perfectly-disciplined will.* If you are low in an area, begin focusing on it today. Consider adopting one characteristic per week. Write it on a card. Look at it hourly. Practice it over and over. By doing this you will become mentally tough and experience Super Bowl success.

---

*Never give up then, for that is just the place and time that the tide will turn.*

—**Harriet Beecher Stowe**

# Work Ethic

WORK ETHIC (wurk eth´ik) n. 1. A willingness to direct rigorous effort or activity toward achieving a goal. The willingness and discipline to apply such effort over a long period of time toward a worthwhile goal. 2. One reason for the Packers' success during the era of Coach Lombardi was that they out-worked their opponents. No, Coach Lombardi never slept in his office as some NFL coaches do today. He went home for dinner every night to be with his family and then returned to the office to resume preparations for the next game. Lombardi's work ethic ensured results. Incidentally, he played hard too. When time allowed, he enjoyed an evening out with close friends. During the off season, he worked just as hard on his golf game as he did on football during the season.

Prisons are full of people who took short-cuts in their effort to achieve success. The thought has always struck me that if these people had worked as hard and as creatively within the law as they did outside it, they would have achieved their goals legitimately. Somewhere these people got the idea they could succeed without effort. In the same way much of society has been misled to believe they are entitled to success without hard work.

Perhaps the media should shoulder part of the blame. In newspapers and television you are constantly shown people who achieve their goals in a seemingly effortless way. This is not the case at all. These people may make it look easy but that's because they enjoy their work. They are in pursuit of a clear, vivid, precise, worthwhile goal. But don't think for a minute that they're not working hard. You cannot achieve success, whatever that means to you, without hard work, application, and dedication. This is true not just in a monetary or material sense. It takes hard work to be a successful spouse and parent. To lead a full balanced, rewarding life takes hard work.—VL, Jr.

---

*The harder you work, the harder it is to surrender.*
—Coach Lombardi

## Work Ethic

HARD work is the parent of all success. A good plan is important. Passionate focus is vital. Technical skill is necessary. However, without hard work it's all meaningless. Most people realize this at a shallow level and will work superficially. But very few are willing to work to the degree necessary for Super Bowl success.

Simply speaking, success is not easy. It requires far more than average effort. Most people are willing to work forty hours a week. That forty hours, even though they may complain, will help you achieve mediocrity. It's extremely difficult to be successful without working beyond the average. For average results, work at an average level. For successful results, you have to work harder and longer than average.

Each ingredient of success discussed up to this point is necessary. They're all vital. A work ethic, however, is the one characteristic that channels the other ingredients towards a goal. Work ethic takes each of the factors and directs them toward success. People who are successful are willing to do things other people will not do. This is the difference. To experience your own success, follow this path. Do the work no one else is willing to do. As a result, you will experience success that no else has experienced. Remember, the difference between champions and contenders is not talent. At the elite level the difference between competitive athletes is minor. Their talent is usually comparable. The gold medal normally goes to the one who worked the hardest, smartest, and longest to achieve the goal. The same appears to be true in all walks of life, from basketball courts to court rooms, the hardest worker usually succeeds. Develop a strong work ethic. It's something anybody can do. You will then experience elite results.

---

*All hard work brings a profit, but mere talk leads only to poverty.*
                    **—Proverbs 14:23** NIV

## Work Ethic

SEVERAL years ago I was teaching a time management seminar. In one segment I was attempting to describe the difference between tasks that are important and those that are merely urgent. Many of the participants complained their days were spent with urgencies. Several, in fact, stated that they could not apply time management because of interruptions and urgent deadlines imposed on them by supervisors.

I let the group discuss the issue and then gave them my response. Each of us has 168 hours in a week. Successful people do not have more hours than others. They simply use them differently. Even people whose job it is to put out fires forty hours a week still have 128 hours. My brother-in-law is a professional firefighter and he is a good one. He works forty-plus hours a week putting out fires. He has another part-time job that consumes another thirty hours a week. You work eight hours a day. You sleep eight hours a night. You still have eight hours left. Manage that eight hours.

Most people look on their careers as something they do for forty hours a week. My belief is that these people will keep up with the Joneses. A few people are willing to go beyond that. These few people have developed a strong work ethic. Their results will always surpass those of the Joneses. Use your time wisely. If your time belongs to someone else, spend it wisely as well. If you are forced to put out fires regularly, don't dismay. You still have a lot of hours left. Remember the difference between where you are and where you want to be is not measured in miles. It's measured in work.—JB

---

*I see no virtue where I smell no sweat.*

—Francis Quarles

## Work Ethic

SUCCESSFUL people are driven by the desire to succeed. However, they aren't *obsessed* with it. These people don't focus narrowly on their success to the exclusion of other important things. When someone becomes obsessed with anything, it is the beginning of his downfall.

Coach Lombardi studied football. He had also attended law school and seminary. He had been a teacher. He was married and had a family. He told his players their priorities should be God first, family second, and the Green Bay Packers third. Coach Lombardi did work hard. His work ethic is legendary. But he wasn't obsessed with winning to the exclusion of everything else.

People who become obsessed burn out very quickly. They lose sight of their health and experience medical problems. They lose sight of their families and experience relationship problems. They often die young as a result of chemical dependency, heart attacks, or suicide. Our motto is *work for success*. Don't become obsessed with it. This week take this baby step. In your journal draw out or design a 168-hour week schedule for your life. Build in somewhere between six to eight hours of sleep a night. Sleep is necessary. If you have a forty hour a week job, fill that in as well. That would leave approximately sixty-four hours a week. Commit yourself to do something in that sixty-four hours a week to contribute to your own journey to success.

---

*I am wondering what would have happened to me if some fluent talker had converted me to the theory of the eight-hour day and convinced me that it was not fair to my fellow workers to put forth my best efforts in my work. I am glad that the eight-hour day had not been invented when I was a young man. If my life had been made up of eight-hour days, I don't believe I could have accomplished a great deal.*
—Thomas Edison

# Life Work

LIFE WORK (lif wurk) n. The chief work of one's lifetime. 2. Contrary to the belief of many, football was not Coach Lombardi's life work. Teaching young athletes at the high school and college level and influencing their character development through the hard lessons of football, was his life work. Lombardi turned to pro football only when his dream of being a college head coach was denied him. Even at the pro level, with players who were supposedly older and wiser, he continued his life work of character development.

I've been associated with a number of people who could be described as successful. It took me awhile before I was able to put my finger on the reason for their success. Of course they practiced the qualities outlined in this book. But mainly it was that their lives were "seamless." In other words, it was impossible to tell where their work left off and the rest of their life began. At first it appeared that they worked all the time. Every activity, no matter the time or the day, had something to do with their work. Then I noticed that for these people work was play. Somehow they had found a way to combine their play with work. If you are one of these people you're very fortunate.

You've probably heard the advice, "Find what you love to do and then figure out a way to make a living doing it." This is wonderful advice. Do it if you can. Unfortunately, by the time many people hear this and they're ready to take it seriously, there are some conflicts. They're called mortgage, maxed-out credit cards, and three teenagers who want to attend private schools. You can't just drop everything to pursue what you love. I love—to read; to take my wife out to dinner; to smoke a good cigar; to listen to smooth jazz; to watch football; to exercise; to take a sauna; to hike. I love to watch a sunrise. I love to see a full moon play across a lake. I don't think anyone wants to pay me to do the things I love. So I work. That's why it's called work. For most of us, work is just one part of our lives. The poetic solution is to see how your work can become a meaningful part of your "life work."—VL, Jr.

---

*I don't think he ever taught me any football. What he'd do three times a week was preach on life.*
—**Henry Jordan,** Defensive Tackle, Green Bay Packers

## Life Work

SIGMUND Freud spent his life studying human behavior. Freud was fascinated with human emotion and motivation. The basis of what is studied today under the headings of psychology, psychiatry, and virtually all behavioral science originated from Freud. He is also widely studied in philosophy. Though many of his early writings have to be looked on more as commentary than science, Freud had incredible insight.

Shortly before his death, Freud was asked what he would claim to be primary elements to happiness. Reportedly, after pausing for a moment of thought, he responded from his hospital bed, "Love and work." It has been suggested that what Freud was really referring to was the work a person perceives as his or her "main calling" in life. Though occasionally that may mean a person's nine-to-five job, in most cases it is not. To some people "work" is something they do to give them the opportunity to pursue their calling. And of course there are the lucky few whose passion, work, and time are spent in the same pursuit.

A *job* is there to produce income. Your *work* may be different than your job. Income may flow from your work if you're lucky. But for most people their *life work* has little to do with their income. Life work is not only healthy, it can be holy. That is the way it was with Coach Lombardi. Remember, your life work may not be your job. My neighbor has a "job" he despises. But he keeps it because it pays well. With that income he is able to conduct his *life work* which is being a youth director at his church. The same principle may apply to you.

---

*You are not here merely to make a living. You are here in order to enable the world to live more amply, with greater vision, with a finer spirit of hope and achievement. You are here to enrich the world, and you impoverish yourself if you forget the errand.*
—Woodrow Wilson

### Life Work

IT'S customary among business people to introduce themselves and identify the company they work for. When I make business-related phone calls there are often receptionists who ask not only my name but who I am *with*. I have gotten a few chuckles by saying that at the time I was alone. However there have been other occasions when I feel mischievous. In personal meetings a man might introduce himself by saying, "I'm Bob, with Bob's Realty." I would say, "Hi, I'm John." Bob would inevitably be in great pain, not knowing exactly where to place me within his particular preconception of occupational status.

I have spent hours speaking to large groups encouraging people not to identify themselves too closely with their jobs. In fact, I would discourage you from identifying too closely with anything over which you have little or no control. Yet, especially with men, it's part of who they are. Many people confuse job and identity. There are a few ways this could conceivably be considered healthy. But the way most people do it, it is not only unhealthy but potentially disastrous.

Recently I have redefined my advice. You may identify with your *work* depending on how you define the concept. However, you are not your *job*. This is especially true if someone else determines how long you keep that job. If you define your work as separate from your job, you could be on to something. To Coach Lombardi his work was helping people. His job was teacher, assistant coach, high school coach, high school teacher, student, etc. However, his work was helping people change and improve their lives. When his *job* changed, his *work* remained the same. That is a good model for each of you.—JB

---

*Do you not see a man skilled in his work? He will serve before kings; he will not serve before obscure men.*

—**Proverbs 22:29** NIV

## Life Work

YOUR willingness to apply a strong work ethic to your *life's work* is an extremely important characteristic. It is of vastly more importance than talent, intelligence or status. Find something you would do for free and make that your life's work. It is probably the best piece of advice I have given anyone, including my own children. When you approach *life's work* this way, it is not work at all.

I have friends who sometimes work sixteen hours a day, six to seven days a week. As a therapist, I worry about them. But usually the closer I get to the person, the more I realize he or she is not working. They are people involved in their life's work. I can't accurately define them as workaholics, because they are not *working* in the classical sense. There is no labor in what they do. It is a joy and a passion. Their life's work generates happiness. When you discover passion in your work, it creates energy and ceases to be a job.

Begin this baby step today. Brainstorm about something you would be willing to do for the rest of your life. Think of several things you would do for free. Ask yourself what gives you the most energy. List them in your journal. Grade the ones which give you the most passion. Narrow the list and experiment with two or three. Then set a time goal at some point in the next ninety days. At that time you will designate what is to be your life's work and begin pursuing it. This doesn't mean you will have to change your job. Your *job* may be something you keep in order to make enough money to pursue your *life's work*. But once you begin, it's only a matter of time before your life work replaces your job. Then you will be well on your way to success.—JB

---

*Have a purpose in life, and having it throw into your work such strength of mind and muscle as God has given you.*
—Thomas Carlyle

# Practice

PRACTICE (prak´tis) n. 1. To exercise or perform repeatedly in order to acquire or polish a skill. 2. The success of Coach Lombardi's Packer offense was predicated on the success of a single play—the "Packer Sweep." The guards and fullback led the halfback in an end sweep. This play had to work so the other plays in the Packer offense could succeed. Coach Lombardi had his offense practice this play repeatedly. As a result, the players gained complete confidence in their ability to execute this single play. Green Bay's opponents and the rest of the world knew the play was coming, yet the Packers still ran it successfully. All successful coaches run the same plays over and over until their players can do it in their sleep. And that's exactly what the coach wants! What the coach doesn't want is for the players to be "thinking" about their next move. If they have to "think" the game will pass them by. What coaches seek to accomplish through practice is a mindset where players act and react instinctively (without thinking).

I average between 70-90 speeches a year. I customize each speech to the audience, yet much of the "good stuff" is the same. I could do most of each speech without a lot of preparation but wouldn't consider it. The audience might not know, but I would. I practice every word of every speech at least twice, even though I've done a lot of it hundreds of times before. The confidence I have as a speaker comes from knowing I've practiced and I'm prepared.

It's the same for everyone. To be successful you have to react not only appropriately, but habitually. This state of mind is reached only by practice. You anticipate the events in your day and mentally practice how you will handle each situation as it arises. With practice you are able to go through each day in a relaxed free-flowing manner. Success is the outcome.—VL, Jr.

---

*You teach discipline by doing it over and over, by repetition and rote, especially in a game like football when you have very little time to decide what you are going to do. So what you do is react almost instinctively, naturally. You have done it so many times, over and over again.*
—Coach Lombardi

Practice

THERE is an old saying common in "pop" psychiatry. "One definition of insanity is doing the same thing over and over again and expecting different results." I believe there is a lot of wisdom in that observation. Another way of saying it would be that it's crazy to practice failure and expect success. Yet this is what most of us do. We repeatedly practice some familiar pattern and merely *wish* for success. It may not be insanity, but it's not the way to become successful.

Coach Lombardi said practice does *not* make perfect. Practice makes permanent. *Perfect* practice makes perfect. If there is a wisdom that most people are missing, this is it. As a psychotherapist, consultant, and speaker, I have spoken to thousands of people over the years. On radio talk shows I have addressed millions of listeners. This is the one obstacle to success I hear echoed regularly. People repeat the same thing over and over again, yet are shocked when the results don't change. If you continue to do something the same way you will get the same results. If you want different results you have to do things differently. For most of us, this is entirely logical but emotionally difficult. It requires you to move outside your comfort zone. It's unfamiliar. It's threatening. It's a problem.

What you practice you become better at. If you practice long enough you actually become that which you practice. It is no longer practice or drill. At this point it is actually who you are. If you want to be a success you need to practice successful principles. Practice baby steps if you want to be a success. Eventually you will become good at it. Practice them even longer and you *will* become successful. It worked for Coach Lombardi, the Green Bay Packers, and hundreds of others. It will work for you as well.—JB

---

*Nobody ever mastered any skill except through intense, persistent and intelligent practice. Practice it the right way.*
                                          —**Norman Vincent Peale**

## Practice

I have several friends who work in emergency rooms. Some are physicians. Some are paramedics. Others are nurses or physicians' assistants. The emergency room is not a place for practice. It is a laboratory where only perfection is allowed. In the crisis mentality of trauma medical care, a minor mistake can result in tragedy, death, or lawsuit. These people feel intense pressure on the job. They are generally unappreciated, yet annually they save millions of lives.

Many of these people run into trouble outside the emergency room. After a number of years they are no longer *practicing* emergency medicine. They have become crisis-oriented. They are *perfectionists*. They often forget that what is true in the emergency room is not necessarily true in the rest of their lives. Most ER patients are there for a serious emergency. A patient enters who has been stabbed in the heart. The well-trained doctor may have to "crack the man's chest" and begin massaging the damaged organ. Hopefully, the patient lives and is passed on to a long-term medical care provider. The emergency provider's job is done and he moves on to the next emergency. That is a crisis-oriented immediate response. But most of life is not like that.

Some emergency medical personnel take this same quick-fix mentality into other phases of their lives. If you have a marriage problem, you can't "crack the chest, massage the heart, and get it going again." If you are having child-rearing problems, a quick fix will not work there either. Yet these caregivers have "practiced" crisis intervention perfectly and expect it to apply universally. Pursue success, but understand most good things take some time. What is true in the emergency room may not be true in all of your life. This is the power of practice. —JB

---

*Be diligent in these matters; give yourself wholly to them, so that everyone may see your progress.*

—1 Timothy 4:15 NIV

Practice

PRACTICE needs to be ongoing. Practice perpetually. Practice tirelessly. Practice at 8 o'clock in the morning, at midday, and the last thing before you go to bed. But make sure you are practicing the right thing in the right way.

You cannot practice too much if you are practicing correctly. Some athletes practice ten hours per day. But they practice intelligently. They break down the requirements of their sport into small sequential skills—*baby steps*. Then they practice each of those steps. They use weight training, simulation, visualization, and mental practice to achieve their mastery. But they ensure they are practicing the right thing in the right way. They have coaches, trainers, and science to back them up.

Take this baby step this week. State your success goal in your journal. Break it down into small achievable components that will take you where you want to go with your life. Begin to practice a series of small skills which, when put together, will help you achieve the success you desire. When you do this, you will be well on your way to success. Remember success is not an incidental phenomenon. It's a result of practicing these small steps the right way for an extended period of time. What you practice you become. But it takes a long time. This kind of practice takes a considerable amount of discipline. There is little or no short-term payoff. But ultimately the practice pays off. You are the skill. It is you. Don't do the same thing over again and expect different results. Do the right thing and practice perfectly.

---

*Only those who have the patience to do simple things perfectly will acquire the skill to do difficult things easily.*
—Johann Christoph von Schiller

# 6

# Developing Attitudes
## of
## Success

*The ability to convert ideas to things is the secret of outward success.*
—Henry Ward Beecher

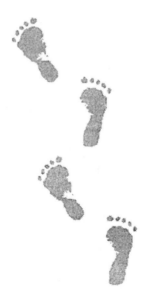

# Desire

DESIRE (di-zir´) v. 1. To wish or long for; want; crave. 2. Coach Lombardi knew that 1967 would be a difficult season for the Packers. They were the oldest team in the NFL. They'd just won their second consecutive championship. It was their fourth in six years. Since even success can become commonplace, Lombardi knew he needed something to rekindle the desire to push for a third championship within his veterans. From the first day of training camp he constantly gave them the challenge of winning three championships in a row. He told them that this would be historic, probably something no team would ever have the opportunity to do again. The championship ring, emblematic of that 1967 season, has three diamonds across the face. They signify those three back-to-back championships. On one side of the ring is the word "Challenge."

I am what is called a "motivational" speaker. Truth be told, I can't motivate anyone. Motivation is internal. It comes from within. As a speaker, what I seek to do is provide good information with a little inspiration and provocation thrown in. For change to take place there must be a spark of inspiration. Goals are important. But there must be a hunger to accomplish the goals. This desire must be constantly fanned.

What it often comes down to is the strength of your desire. You need to have so much desire that the gain becomes worth the pain. You can pay lip service to your goal, or your desire for success can be so strong that you're willing to sacrifice for it. There's nothing wrong if at this moment you don't have this burning desire. You just don't have a goal that has captured your heart and imagination. You have a choice. You can continue to live today the same as yesterday. Or you can choose a goal that ignites the fire of desire within you and begin to live as your creator intended.—VL, Jr.

---

*I'd rather have a player with 50% ability and 100% desire because the guy with 100% desire you know is going to play every day so you can make the system to fit into what he can do. The other guy—the guy with the 100% ability and 50% desire—can screw up your whole system because one day he'll be out there waltzing around.*
—Coach Lombardi

Desire

JUST for the sake of discussion, let's say success is a game like football. To be successful in football you have to have the technical skill, the physical conditioning, and practice. To be a success at *success* you must have the same elements. However, there is one missing component. To be successful at football you have to know the rules. Knowing the rules of baseball won't help you play football. In the same way to be *successful* you must know the rules. And most people don't.

Coach Lombardi knew both the rules of football and the rules of success. What worked for him can work for you as well. One of the things Coach Lombardi preached was the need for ambition and desire. He taught that desire creates the fire of success. It fuels success. It's probably not surprising that the people who experience the most success are those who desire it. They learn the rules of the game and they learn the rules of success. They follow the formula precisely. They're not always the smartest, best educated, or most athletic. However they do desire success more than their peers.

The truth is, regardless of where you are at this moment, you can experience success. The Packers were perennial cellar dwellers when they began practicing these principles. Even if your career is at a low or you're in an emotional cellar you *can* begin to experience success. You must desire it. And you must desire it with passion, energy, and intensity. You must desire success like you never desired anything else before. It worked for the Packers and it will work for you as well.

---

*I hope that I may always desire more than I can accomplish.*
—Michelangelo

## Desire

SUCCESS doesn't keep a schedule. It's not seasonal. It doesn't care about your gender, race, or age. Success in the free-enterprise system is an equal-opportunity phenomenon. It does not discriminate on any basis. Success only discriminates against those who fail to desire it.

I have a friend who experienced a life change in his late fifties. He'd been a foreign missionary since his early twenties. He had experienced success in his "mission" but had little interest in financial accomplishment. After a series of tragedies, including the death of one of his children, he left the mission field and began living a different life. This man, who in many ways was a "Mother Teresa" figure, decided he wanted to experience a different side of life. We had a discussion about his decision and I gave him copies of the early ideas for this book. He agreed to use them in his new goal of achieving financial success.

This experiment began four years before this book was published. In that four-year period he has literally amassed a small fortune. He followed all the rules and practiced them tirelessly. But he said it was his *desire* to achieve financially that truly made the difference. "It energized me," he explained. "I had a lot of doubt initially and there were a lot of struggles along the way for a man of my age. But the desire and ambition were far more powerful than my doubts. That carried me when the going got rough." That's the power of desire. It creates fire. It worked for Coach Lombardi and the Green Bay Packers. It worked for my friend who had no experience with financial success at all. And it will work for you. You need to desire your goal for success. You have to actually establish success as a destination. Visualizations, planning, and all the other steps are necessary. However if you *desire* something intensely enough and follow through on the other steps, nothing will stand in your way.—JB

---

*You can have anything you want if you want it desperately enough. You must want it with an inner exuberance that erupts through the skin and joins the energy that created the world.*

—Sheila Graham

## Desire

THE opposite of ambition is not laziness. It's apathy. Unfortunately, it's too easy to grow stagnant with the status quo. People too readily lose the desire to improve their lives and be successful. Once desire leaves, the fuel for change is gone. Once apathy sets in, you can be overcome by the amotivational syndrome.

People then act as if their life is meaningless and irrelevant. They have lost the confidence to try or even attempt improving their situation. They quit trying because they don't believe success is possible. They give up and spend their time escaping. Sometimes this escape can take the form of alcoholism or drug abuse. At other times escape is accomplished through television or food. They live vicariously and experience success by passively watching their favorite sports teams on TV. When their team loses, they get upset and whine to any talk radio host who will listen. When their team wins, they feel victorious. Their lives revolve around their *pastime* instead of their *passion*. And they have few, if any, goals of their own. They *desire* only to make it to the next game or the next season. All of these outlets are "drugs" and are highly addictive.

Take this baby step this week. Begin to visualize yourself having a burning desire and ambition to succeed. Visualize how you would appear if you had this burning desire. What would you wear? How would you walk? How would you talk? Who would you associate with? What would you read or listen to? What would you do with your free time? Answer each of these questions in your journal and then begin living this way today. Act "as if" you are the person who had achieved that goal. Do as Jim Cathcart suggested. Ask, "How would the person I wish to become react in this situation?" Then do whatever that person would do. Try it for twenty-eight days. Remember, desire burns internally. The fire of desire must come from within. But the flame is ignited externally. It can be ignited by answering the questions in this paragraph and doing what the answers suggest.

---

*The desire accomplished is sweet to the soul.*
—Proverbs 13:19a

# Visualize

VISUALIZE (vizh´oo-a-liz) v. 1. To form a mental image or vision of; to envision. 2. The concept of visualization wasn't widely known in the 1960's. Yet in his own way Coach Lombardi practiced visualization. What Lombardi did was run difficult, stress-filled practices, that covered every contingency the upcoming game might present to his team. By Sunday, the players had "seen" every situation they would face during the game. And it was in as stressful an environment as the game itself. In a very real sense, the manner in which the Packers practiced during the week presented them with a visual preview of the stress and ever-changing conditions they would face on Sunday.

*Psycho-Cybernetics* by Maxwell Maltz was a revelation to me. This book led me to other self-help books and tapes as I steeped myself in the science of personal growth. From the very start, however, there remained the ever-present question of how to apply this information. The answer was in visualization. Athletics have provided most of the research on visualization. Elite athletes practice a technique called rehearsal visualization. They visualize themselves performing key elements of the sport in a flawless manner. Since the subconscious doesn't know the difference between a real and a vividly imagined experience, you can practice perfectly in your mind. It's as effective as if the event actually happened.

The challenge is to apply this technique to your quest for success. You need to study the concepts in this book, then internalize and implement them in your daily life. Practice rehearsal visualization daily. Rehearse being successful. As you continue to do this on a regular, disciplined basis, you begin to develop that quiet confidence that comes from knowing you are on the road to success.—VL, Jr.

---

*I don't think any team went into its game each Sunday as well prepared as we were. We knew just what to expect and we knew just how to cope with it.*
      —**Paul Hornung,** Hall of Fame Halfback, Green Bay Packers

## Visualize

I am not a connoisseur of movies. I enjoy watching them occasionally, usually on home video. Many movies are too boring and predictable. I am usually unaffected by them. Yet there are several glaring exceptions to this generality.

The first movie that truly affected me was a Hitchcock thriller. Then there was the first release of *Jaws* many years ago. I had a similar reaction to *The Towering Inferno* which came out about the same time. More recently I had an unusual reaction to *Silence of the Lambs*. It hypnotized me. My blood pressure soared. My heart rate skyrocketed and I experienced authentic fear. I think this reaction occurred because each of these movies left a great deal to the imagination.

Alfred Hitchcock was the master of this. There was actually little violence in Hitchcock's thrillers. Much was implied but little was actually shown. *Silence of the Lambs* followed this formula precisely. The viewer was left to imagine the true horror that Hannibal Lector embodied. Hitchcock had an incredible respect for imagination. He realized viewers could mentally picture far more frightening images than he could ever portray. This is the power of visualization. This is the power of mental practice. When producing his movies, Hitchcock would visualize each and every component of the movie from various angles and various dimensions. He realized that the brain reacts more powerfully to that which is imagined than to that which is real. Mental practice can be used to entertain you. It can also be used to improve your performance. It is a skill common among all successful people.—JB

---

*Assume in your imagination it is already yours, the goal you aspire to have; enter into the part enthusiastically, live the character just as does the great actor absorb the character he plays.*
—Ralph Waldo Emerson

## Visualize

SOMETIMES you have to "see it to believe it." This sort of mental practice or visualization is best accomplished multi-dimensionally. It helps to actually see, hear, taste, touch, feel, and experience your success goal. You also need to see it from beginning to end as if you had already achieved it beforehand. The process of actually achieving your success then becomes simply an afterthought.

Several years ago I worked with a high school wrestling team teaching them mental practice skills. One young man had experienced a promising career as a wrestler but had never won a state championship. I visited with him privately several times prior to the state tournament. We would go through a visualization exercise and actually imagine the tournament from the beginning to end. He saw every aspect of the tournament, in addition to himself actually winning the matches. Prior to the semifinal and final matches I visited with him personally at the gymnasium and helped him do more visualization. This mental conditioning worked for him. It can work for you in your "tournament" as well.

Some say visualization is more powerful than physical practice. Others say it actually attracts success. In this young man's case it was true. He won the state championship. I remember the first words he said to me when we were celebrating. "It's just like you said." He smiled, "It's like I had been there before. I had already won before I even stepped out on the mat. I just had to go through the motions of winning. My head was that convinced." It worked in wrestling. It worked for the Green Bay Packers. It can work for you.—JB

---

*. . . old men will dream dreams . . . young men will see visions.*
—Joel 2:28 NIV

Visualize

VISUALIZE until you realize. Success can be a long journey. Inspiration can arise from experiencing your success mentally before you have actually experienced it physically. Since the mind does not know the difference between that which is imagined and that which is real you can become conditioned to success through visualizing it before you actually experience it. This can actually help you realize the success you desire much more rapidly.

To visualize, begin by vividly imagining the desired result. This is best accomplished by sitting in a calm and peaceful environment. Close your eyes and actually see and experience in your mind what it would be like to be successful in your chosen endeavor. The more senses you use the better. See, hear, taste, touch, smell, and experience the goal. Most people find a minimum of ten minutes daily will get you started. Science, philosophy, and experience all agree that visualization is vital to your success.

Take this baby step this week. Begin to visualize your goal. Visualize success as you define it. Do this as described for a minimum of ten minutes daily beginning today. It will speed you on your journey to success. Remember, the more comprehensive your visualization the better. Find a place where you won't be distracted. Sit comfortably with your back erect. Shut your eyes and touch the tip of your tongue to the roof of your mouth. Place your hands in your lap and touch the tips of your middle finger and thumb together. Breathe deeply inhaling through your nose and exhaling slowly through your mouth. Then begin to imagine yourself achieving your goal. See, hear, taste, touch and smell it. See it as though you have already succeeded. See yourself in possession of that success. Experience it. This process is very powerful and will help you realize your goal.

---

*What I desire I must first sense. What I sense I create.*
                                        —**Michelangelo**

# Attitude

ATTITUDE (at´e-tood´) n. 1. A state of mind as in *positive* attitude. A state of mind that positive results can and will flow from all things. 2. As a member of a profession where job performance was recorded on scoreboards, Coach Lombardi was aware of the possibility of losing. He never conceded it could happen to him. When he took over the team in Green Bay, he told the players he had never been part of a losing team and didn't intend to start. The players quickly adopted Lombardi's attitude. With a confidence borne of superb physical conditioning and thorough preparation the Packers never felt they "lost" a game. Once in a while however, they did run out of time.

Occasionally I give seminars on negotiations. I did quite a lot of negotiating when I worked in professional football. One thing I emphasize when speaking on negotiation is body language. Good negotiators understand it is the strongest indicator of people's attitudes. The person sitting across from you during a negotiation may be saying one thing while their body language is sending a different message. The body *does* what the mind is *thinking.*

Think back to the last time you felt out of place, or didn't know anyone. Perhaps you crossed your arms across your chest or assumed the "fig leaf" position, with your hands together just below your waist. When you feel threatened, you instinctively cover up vulnerable areas like your lungs, heart, stomach, and groin. Conversely, when you feel confident. You freely assume the position of command—hands behind your back, in a General Patton pose. If you're really confident, you put your hands on your hips in a "let's have some action" stance. The next time you feel confidence ebbing and catch yourself covering up your core area of vulnerability—stop. Assume the position of command, place your hands on your hips. You will be surprised how this change in body language will bring about a subtle change in your attitude. You can change your attitude by changing your body language!—VL, Jr.

---

*I never tell a football team anything that I don't absolutely believe myself. I always tell them the truth. I can't even try to deceive them, because they'd know. I'd know, so they'd know.*
—Coach Lombardi

## Attitude

OVER the past several years the term "attitude" has taken on a negative meaning. If someone is described as having an *attitude* it is the same thing as saying that person is sarcastic or in some way negative. That is not the way the term was originally intended and certainly not the way it is listed in the dictionary.

Having a positive attitude means you seize the moment and then ask what you can do to make it better. It's making the most of what is given to you. A positive attitude results in your using the available time in a way that leads to success. It can be developed. It can be learned. A positive outlook is not something you're born with. It's one of the greatest assets on the journey to success. Your attitude not only *affects* outcome it can *determine* it. Regardless of the attitude you have today, a positive one can be yours.

A positive attitude will help you look on the bright side of everything. Your most negative comment will become, "What can I learn from this?" Failure will come to be redefined as a mistake. Mistakes will be interpreted as learning experiences and all learning will be vie  .d as opportunity. Simply put, a positive attitude will lead to you making something constructive out of whatever adversity you face. Make no mistake about it, you will face difficulty. The road to success is littered with obstacles. With a positive attitude, obstacles are not magically or mystically transformed. They are simply negotiated. You go over, under, around, or through them instead of giving up or quitting. As a result, something positive always happens eventually.

---

*The greatest discovery of my generation is that a human being can alter his life by changing his attitude.*
—William James

## Attitude

WILLIAM James said, "Emotion is not always immediately subject to reason but it is subject to action." It is important to realize that you can't always change what you are doing by waiting for your attitude to change. But you can change your attitude by changing your *actions*. Few people are mentally strong enough to initially create a change in their attitude. With most people, it takes a change in action first to jump-start an emotional metamorphosis.

As an experiment I asked a person in counseling how he would act if he were happy. After he hesitated, I had him make a list of all the things he would do if he were not depressed. I then asked how he would act and what he would do if he had a positive attitude. He made another list of all the things he would be doing if that were the case. We then developed a schedule for him in his day planner and he committed to do all of the things he had listed earlier. He scheduled each at a particular time every day for a period of two weeks. The key was that he cooperated with this experiment. He was willing to complete everything on the list. Most people aren't. He wasn't looking for a magic pill like most people. Instead he was looking for change. It was not only a matter of emotion, it was a matter of employment. If he didn't change, he would lose his job.

Predictably, it worked. The changes in attitude followed his change in action. His employer noticed. His wife was shocked. Friends asked what had happened. People began to compliment him and tell him how much better he looked. A few even asked if he was on drugs! He was on drugs all right. He was *high* from focusing on action rather than emotions. This is a specific reflection of what William James said many years ago. Attitude may not be immediately subject to reason. But it is subject to action. Do you want to change your attitude? Change what you are doing today.—JB

---

*For as he thinketh in his heart, so is he.*

—**Proverbs 23:7**

## Attitude

MANY years ago William Shakespeare said, "Our doubts are traitors and make us lose the good we oft might win, by fearing to attempt." Your fears and doubts are not your friends. Shakespeare said they are traitors, and Coach Lombardi would say they are your opponent. There will be a constant struggle, perhaps for the rest of your life, over who ultimately wins.

The fact is if your mind obsesses on your doubts, fears, or disbelief, you will move toward them. If your mind fixates on the positive, you'll move in that direction. Don't make the mistake of focusing on what you "don't want." If you focus on your fears or doubts, you will experience them as the outcome. If you focus on your goals and your dreams with a positive attitude, you will experience them instead.

Take this baby step today. Make a list in your journal of your gravest doubts and your worst fears. Write about each of them comprehensively. Ensure there is nothing in your mind that is not on your piece of paper. After you have exhaustively listed each doubt or fear, write at least a page about each one. As an example, if you doubt your intelligence, explain your feelings. Describe them in detail. Discuss how you arrived at the low assessment of your intellect. Make a list of the various ways you have been affected by this doubt. What has it "cost" you in terms of missed opportunity? What could you gain by overcoming this doubt? What do you stand to lose by not changing your opinion? How would your life improve if this doubt was removed? Discuss each of these questions in detail and write anything else you think might be important. Afterwards develop some strategies to begin creating change. It will take a while. But you've got the rest of your life as a payoff.

---

*All that a man achieves and all that he fails to achieve is the direct result of his own thoughts.*

—James Allen

## Optimism

OPTIMISM (op´te-miz´em) n. 1. A tendency to expect the best possible outcome, or to dwell on the most hopeful aspects of a situation. 2. Coach Lombardi was genuinely optimistic. His optimism was a necessity. If he lacked it, so would his players. Football games are rarely won by those who don't believe they can win. Because he worked so closely with his players, they came to know one another very well. Lombardi couldn't fake it. His optimism had to be real. If it wasn't the players would know.

When my kids were young, I often responded to their complaints by saying, "Where is it written that life should be fair?" I asked once too often because one of them replied, "On the refrigerator." Sure enough, on the refrigerator was a big handwritten sign, "Life should be fair!" But it's not. "Stuff" happens, and how you deal with life's misfortunes is up to you. It will be easier if you choose to deal with life optimistically.

Many of us are optimistic about the big things. The economy will continue to perform well. Elected officials in Washington aren't going to do us too much harm. Our favorite baseball team has a chance to win the World Series. Sales are going well, so the job seems secure. Our kids are going to turn out to be responsible adults one day. See, I'm optimistic! But what about the smaller things in your life? When you leave the house in the morning to drive to work, do you just know the traffic will be backed up for miles? When you go to the grocery store, are you resigned to the fact that there won't be a parking place? When you go out for dinner, do you just know there will be a forty-five minute wait? And do you just know it will rain on your day off? As these little negatives accumulate, they add up. They wear you out and drain you of energy. And optimism is about energy. The more optimistic you are, the more energy you have. Optimistic people have a bounce in their step that you can almost see. They blow past life's little frustrations. Half the problems we anticipate never occur, but the energy we waste worrying about them grinds us down. Be optimistic about the small things in your life and the big things have a way of taking care of themselves.—VL, Jr.

---

*It is essential to understand that battles are primarily won in the hearts of men.*

—Coach Lombardi

## Optimism

COACH Lombardi's life was not without setbacks. One of his greatest obstacles came from the sport which he loved. It came from football itself. He struggled for twenty years before becoming a professional head football coach. He was a coach at the high school and collegiate level. He was assistant NFL coach for the New York Giants for years. But his goal of becoming head coach eluded him. Coach Lombardi felt discriminated against because he was both Italian and Catholic. There had never been an Italian or Catholic head coach in the history of the sport.

Lombardi's own brand of optimism kept him going. Optimism is the way you perpetually interpret and explain things that happen to you. This is especially true for roadblocks and obstacles. Pessimism is psychologically fatal. It is emotionally infectious. And since the mind and body are inseparably connected, it should be no surprise that people who are not optimistic experience more health problems, physical illness, and depression.

The truth is you don't have control over most things in life. But you can control your degree of optimism. You can't change the weather when it rains on your parade. But you can determine how you are going to respond to the rain. You can speed your passage toward optimism by doing the following things. First, take great pains to disagree with any negative thought you have. You will experience negative thoughts from time-to-time. When you do, either disagree with them or dismiss them. Next, practice optimism, even if it is visualization and mental practice. Practice it mentally first and you will be able to experience it later. Remember to reward small steps to becoming optimistic. Each time you experience an optimistic thought, praise yourself. Finally, continually set optimistic goals. For example, make it a daily goal to listen to an inspirational cassette. Make a daily goal to read something positive. Make a daily goal to meditate or have a positive thinking period. By doing this, you will have a faster journey on your way to success.

---

*It is the mind that maketh good of ill, that maketh wretch of happy, rich or poor.*

—Edmund Spenser

## Optimism

AFTER one speaking engagement, I was listening to a discussion among several people in the audience. I try to listen after conducting a speaking engagement. Everyone has spent time listening to me. I think it is appropriate that I listen to them. On this particular occasion the man I was listening to was friendly. Yet it was obvious he was miserable.

He was explaining how he had grown up feeling pessimistic about life. He described his entire family as melancholy. They always looked at the most tragic and malignant interpretation of any event. He seemed to think this was genetic. He even claimed he had inherited this negative point of view from both sets of parents and grandparents.

After listening to him to the point of discomfort, I finally interrupted. I gently explained that what he was describing was not genetic. He attempted to disagree. I quickly sidetracked him by asking if both his parents spoke English. He said they did. I then suggested it wasn't genetic that he spoke English. It was simply that he had learned to do so. In the same way, he had also learned to speak a melancholy emotional language. I suggested that his pessimism was not inherited but learned. In the same way he could learn to be more optimistic. He could learn to put a different interpretation on events that happened to him. When he asked how, I answered, "the same way we begin to speak English—by listening to tapes, positive literature, going to seminars—exposing yourself to a new language." I encouraged him not to abandon his family, but at the same time not to expose himself to negative people or discussions unnecessarily. I make the same suggestion to anyone who struggles with habitual negativism. In fact I encourage you to do the same.—JB

---

*A merry heart doeth good like a medicine: but a broken spirit drieth the bones.*

—**Proverbs 17:22**

Optimism

PEOPLE with an optimistic point of view do suffer setbacks, but they see them as only temporary. They do not interpret setbacks as reflecting something inherently wrong with them. They see them as situations only. A setback is something to learn from. These people understand the setback. They accept it. They ask what they can learn from it. Then they ask what to *do* next.

People with an optimistic point of view have an inherent sense of self-worth. This too is something they have learned. As a result of this belief they have a high degree of hope for the future. This leads them to achieve beyond what others may achieve. It also results in achieving beyond what they themselves might otherwise hope for. People with a high degree of optimism and self-belief are willing to make attempts even in the face of adversity.

Take this baby step today. Think about mistakes you have made in the past. Ask yourself, "What did I learn from these setbacks?" List them in your journal. Then closely monitor any negative self-talk in the future. In fact, the most critical thing you should say to yourself is, "What do I *need to learn* from this setback?" If necessary, rephrase the question so it will work for you. Memorize it and get in the habit of using it when otherwise you would kick yourself. "What do I need to learn from this setback?" Practice it until it becomes a part of you and then use it wisely. Remember, pessimism is learned. Misery is learned. Failure is learned as well. The good news is, so is success. Begin learning it today.

---

*An obvious fact about negative feelings is often overlooked. They are caused by us, not by exterior happenings. An outside event presents the challenge, but we react to it. So we must attend to the way we take things, not to the things themselves.*

—Vernon Howard

# 7

# Learning to Stay on the Road to Success

*A minute's success pays the failure of years.*
—Robert Browning

## Continuous Improvement

CONTINUOUS IMPROVEMENT (kon-tin´yoo-es im-proov´ment) n. 1. An unceasing act of advancing to a better state or quality. A mind set, or way of thinking. Believing you can get better and your performance can improve at each step along the way. 2. For the Green Bay Packers the overall transition from a poor team with a record of 1-10-1 to a good team with a record of 7-5 was rather quick. But Coach Lombardi understood that for his team to become a dominant one it would take longer and be far more difficult. His approach was to take baby steps, where every day, for every player, the goal was to be better than yesterday. Every week, the goal was to be better than last week, and every season the goal was to be better than the previous one.

I'm a better speaker than I was 8 years ago. I'm a better husband than I was 32 years ago. Changes like this take place so slowly, so subtly, as to be almost unnoticed. Often we're not even aware that we've changed. Someone else, usually someone close to us, needs to point it out before we notice.

Lasting change is incremental. It is a process of continuous improvement. There are no overnight successes. Show me an overnight success and I'll show you a lot of work that took place out of sight. Nowhere is the concept of baby steps more appropriate than continuous improvement. If your goals are too big you may get discouraged at how far you have to travel to achieve them. You may get impatient and frustrated at your lack of progress. This is natural. This frustration can be converted into the energy you need to pursue your goals a little harder. Don't get discouraged. See success as a process of slow, steady, continuous improvement. It's a baby step to success.—VL, Jr.

---

*All he [Coach Lombardi] wanted from you was perfection.*
—Jim Taylor, Fullback, Green Bay Packers

## Continuous Improvement

AT the close of WWII the Japanese economy and infrastructure was in ruins. Their society had been destroyed industrially, militarily and emotionally. The people were devastated. If ever there was a time for success principles that really worked, this was it. They had everything to gain and nothing to lose.

General Douglas McArthur was given the task of rebuilding post-WWII Japan. It turned out to be an unpopular decision domestically but an ingenious one internationally. To assist him McArthur recruited W. Edwards Deming who at the time was an unknown, unrespected, and under-employed American consultant. His work began. It was a true example of the *phoenix* myth. Literally from the ashes of nuclear devastation, a new nation arose. And it was definitely far stronger and more imposing than its predecessor. Many people still remember sarcastic jokes about the label *"Made in Japan."* It was a sure sign of inferiority. Their reputation obviously changed rapidly. Who won WWII? Maybe the country who first listened and adopted Deming's principles.

One of Deming's primary concepts was that of continuous and constant improvement. In my opinion, this was his most important idea. There's always a better way. The Japanese embraced Deming's principles and made them their own. Continuous improvement in Japanese is called *kaizan*. But it is not Japanese at all. It came from Deming via Douglas McArthur. These two men, both of whose ideas were rejected by Americans, found a willing audience in Japan. As a result, the world has never been the same. Continuous improvement can work for you the same way it worked for them. An interesting footnote: As an assistant coach at West Point, one of Lombardi's weekly tasks was to take the game films to General McArthur's home and discuss the game. We can only wonder about their discussions and McArthur's impact on the young Coach Lombardi. Surely the topic of *kaizan* arose!

---

*Surrounded by a forest of enemies' spears, enter deeply and you learn to use your mind as a shield.*

—Morihei Ueshiba

## Continuous Improvement

OVER the past fifteen years Deming's principles have been practiced—but predominately distorted—by Americans. Continuous improvement and Deming's ideas in general have been scapegoated as the reason for downsizing and other excuses for cutbacks. This was not what Dr. Deming had in mind. The Japanese not only adopted Deming's principles but embraced all of them. Deming spoke about far more than continuous improvement applied to manufacturing and industry. He also talked about how it applies to people.

According to Deming, continuous improvement was not only important to the manufacturing process but also to human relationships. This is why Japanese workers are given lifetime employment. It also explains why many Japanese are willing to work so hard they die for their companies. Many literally work themselves to death. There is even a word for it. It's called *kiroshi*. *Kiroshi* is a result of the incredible commitment they feel toward their organizations, not because of the fear of receiving a pink slip.

In Japan continuous improvement is a way of life. It affects the way they tend their gardens. It's reflected in the way they drink tea. It is seen in the pride and honor they show in their martial arts. You *continuously improve* whatever it is you do until it becomes an art form unto itself. In Japan martial arts are truly arts. In many other countries it's only a way of learning how to fight. There is a vast difference. Recently the Japanese economy has been threatened. Their own economists have given fascinating explanations. They blame certain business executives for placing profit before people. One commentator explained they have ignored Deming's "most important principle."

---

*No pain, no palm; no thorns, no throne; no gall, no glory; no cross, no crown.*

—William Penn

Continuous Improvement

WITH this philosophy there grows a belief that there is always a better way. It's not reinventing the wheel but improving the currently existing one. Life is a long series of learning experiences. It is a continuous process, not a plateau that can be reached. There is a better way to do everything. Continuous improvement also means continuous *self-improvement*. There is no such thing as too much knowledge, too much happiness, or too much success. It's a process, not a plateau.

Take this baby step beginning today. In your journal divide your life into different areas. As an example, it may be the areas of personal growth, financial growth, spiritual growth, family growth and marriage, or primary relationship growth. Each day choose an area and write down one specific thing you can do to improve that aspect of your life. Do this for a period of three weeks. It will speed your journey to success.

Remember, continuous improvement and perfectionism are not the same thing. Continuous improvement is utilizing the finished product while simultaneously studying ways to make it even better. Perfectionism is stalling the finished product indefinitely, maybe even forever. After all, it's not *perfect*. The problem is, it never will be. *Continuous improvement* does not worry about being perfect. It focuses on function and improving function. Perfectionism is immobilizing. Continuous improvement puts you on the road to success. Perfectionism is a crippling disease. Continuous improvement is empowering. Perfectionism will destroy you. Continuous improvement will strengthen you. Start today.

―――――――――

*I have learned that success is to be measured not so much by the position that one has reached in life as by the obstacles which he has overcome while trying to succeed.*
                                        —Booker T. Washington

# Learning

LEARNING (lur´ning) n. 1. Acquired wisdom, knowledge, or skill. 2. Despite spending sixteen hours a day on football, Coach Lombardi possessed surprising breadth and depth. He kept himself well informed on current events and eagerly engaged friends in discussing religion, politics, philosophy, and the social implications of the day's events. It was obvious to those around him that he was continually learning from each day's experiences.

A favorite affirmation of mine is, "I'm either getting what I want or it is a lesson." Life is a series of lessons. We either accomplish a goal today, or falling short, learn something that can be put to good use tomorrow. Many successful people take a little time before bed to take stock of the day just passed. They spend a few minutes going over what they accomplished and reflecting on what they might have learned. This puts the day behind them, helps them sleep restfully and provides a good start to the next morning. This could work for you as well. Give it a try.

Of course, learning encompasses more than what life's experiences can teach you. Successful people see themselves as lifetime students. Whatever your preferred method of learning—reading, listening, watching—do it. Read books, listen to tapes, and watch educational programs. The most successful people are the most vigorous students. They waste little time, even in entertainment. Everything they do—even leisure—is purposeful. They are continually learning from each experience and the people they associate with. The day you stop learning is the day you stop living.—VL, Jr.

---

*He (Coach Lombardi) made us all better than we thought we could be.*
—**Jerry Kramer,** Offensive Guard, Green Bay Packers

## Learning

IT'S fascinating to investigate the mind of a successful person. These people are quick to focus, usually unclouded in their thinking, and satisfied, but always looking for more. Successful people enjoy the status quo but are always searching for ways to improve their lives. Their minds are open, not judgmental or narrow. They're responsive to learning from people and opportunity. They also have incredible perseverance.

Coach Lombardi was successful as a high school and college football coach. He even coached baseball and basketball in high school. Though he was satisfied with his success at the high school level, he wanted more. When the opportunity came to coach at Fordham he took advantage of it. He continued to persevere and eventually joined the ranks of the pro coaches. And even though it took longer than he actually wanted, he didn't give up. Coach Lombardi continued to focus and eventually rose to the helm of the Green Bay Packers.

Successful people enjoy learning. They seek every opportunity to learn. The biggest mistake unsuccessful people make is in missing such opportunities. Emerson said, " . . . to the dull mind all nature is leaden. To the illuminated mind the whole world burns and sparkles with light." It was true for Emerson. Let it be true for you. Open your mind to opportunities around you and you will have far more success. You will also become far more flexible and responsive. Don't wait. Begin today.

---

*Make every effort to add to your faith goodness; and to goodness, knowledge; and to knowledge, self control; and to self control, perseverance; . . . For if you possess these qualities in increasing measure, they will keep you from being ineffective and unproductive.*
                                                    —2 Peter 1:5-8a

## Learning

MANY years ago I was a guest on a radio talk show. During this show I was asked about the distinguishing characteristics of high achievers. The fact is they have several things in common. The first one is they make their work look easy. Most of us miss the reality that they have spent countless hours in preparation and training for their work. It is estimated that most high achievers work sixty hours per week for twenty years before they reach their pinnacle. That's a minimum of 60,000 hours learning their craft. And it is the 60,000 hours that makes it look easy.

The minds of high achievers are well developed because of the many hours they've devoted to their work. As a result they make it look effortless. But it's not. The 60,000 hours invested in learning their craft makes the difference. All that most of us see is the final effort. And the final effort looks easy. The Green Bay Packers made football look easy. Bart Starr's passes to Carroll Dale were a work of perfect choreography. The sweeps, with Paul Hornung following Fuzzy Thurston, Jerry Kramer, and Jim Taylor, look more like a fine-tuned machine than people. The Packers epitomized the team concept, but it wasn't easy. It was from hours and hours of learning.

Many people aren't willing to make the investment in time that such learning requires. But you can be different. Instead of fantasizing about how brilliant someone else is, develop your own genius. Spend the hours and talent will follow. It is not found in IQ. It's found in the hours of learning and polishing your craft. Learning has little to do with intelligence or talent. It's spending the time. All high achievers do it. So can you.—JB

---

*The more I learn the more I realize I don't know, and the more I realize I don't know the more I want to learn.*

—**Albert Einstein**

Learning

ALVIN Toffler wrote the book *Future Shock*. He was a prophet. He truly foresaw our future. Knowledge doubles every five years today. Most people can't keep up and "future shock" strikes regularly. To be successful your mind needs to be able to absorb, adapt, and change rapidly. To do anything else is to self-destruct.

Increase your own learning curve. Attend seminars, read books, and listen to tapes. Do each of these things aggressively and regularly as a way of keeping your mind in shape. It needs a workout just as your body does. Your mind can become flabby if not exercised properly. Stretch it continuously. This usually requires going outside your comfort zone and trying new things. A "new thing" doesn't have to be something experimental. It definitely isn't anything high risk or dangerous. Learning is environmentally friendly and recyclable! It can be summed up in a few simple words. Learn something new!

Today take this baby step. Start your own perpetual learning program. Purchase or borrow books and tapes. Find out about local seminars. Call nearby community colleges and ask them to send you continuing education catalogs and to keep you on their mailing list. Stretch your mind. It will never revert back to its previous shape. Remember, acquire learning material that will help improve your life. Utilize the material listed in the resource section of the book. It will speed your journey on the way to happiness.

---

*If a little knowledge is dangerous, where is the man who has so much as to be out of danger?*
—Thomas Henry Huxley

# Struggle

STRUGGLE (strug´el) v. 1. A testing period, occasionally lasting a great length of time that is rewarded by success for those who don't quit. 2. Every game Coach Lombardi's teams lost was a disappointment. Lombardi wanted to win every game, of course. But he welcomed an occasional defeat because it provided him with the opportunity to refocus the players and take them back to the basics. Lombardi felt it was easier to motivate his players after a defeat, because after they failed he had their undivided attention.

History is full of examples of people who struggle before succeeding. Invariably, these people will tell you that it was the struggles and disappointments that made their success not only possible, but all the more satisfying. Life goes on after a failure. Life goes on with or without you. Adversity, suffering, failure, and disappointment are a vital part of life. Life is a test. Fortunately, you get to grade yourself. You pass the test in terms of how you've turned failed attempts into success.

There was a time in my life when I was depressed over a set-back. I had lost a re-election bid to the Minnesota House of Representatives. I was disappointed because I had lost and I was downright depressed that the logical thing for me to do was to return to the practice of law—which I didn't want to do. But with four children and a mortgage I didn't see any alternative. I don't know if I was clinically depressed, but things appeared so bleak as to be black. I spent hours pacing the parking lot outside my office groping for a solution. More importantly, I steeped myself in self-help books, trying to rekindle within myself the enthusiasm I knew I needed to push ahead. This is a process I have subsequently followed after every struggle. It took nearly a year, but with the support of my wife, I pulled myself together. It had been a year of doubt and second guesses. As a result, today I am a better person.—VL, Jr.

---

*In great attempts, it is glorious even to fail.*

—Coach Lombardi

## Struggle

THE quote at the bottom of this page is one of my all-time favorites. J. W. N. Sullivan certainly had the right idea. Suffering is not simply to polish one's creativity. It is necessary for personality development. Perhaps I embrace Sullivan so closely because of my own struggles. Or maybe because it is one of my values. Perhaps it's the sheer poetry of Sullivan's words. Nevertheless, I believe he is correct.

There is evidence of this throughout history. The Bible is filled with examples of how struggle resulted in heroics. David's problems, the story of Moses, and various New Testament parables illustrate the same point. Similarly, the story of Abraham Lincoln demonstrates the same idea. Here is a man who had lost seven political races before becoming president. He struggled with severe depression and loneliness as well. There are similar stories of business leaders and multi-millionaires who, although they endured bankruptcies, nervous breakdowns, and countless family problems, lived through their struggles and prospered in the end.

I may be a fanatic on this point. But I believe struggle is the "breakfast of champions." It strengthens your character. Your very existence necessitates struggles. And perhaps, as Sullivan suggests, it's the purpose of evil. It builds life muscles. It will help you be more successful as well. Don't run away from necessary suffering. It will catch you and punish you even more. Face it. Appreciate it. And you will be successful.—JB

---

*To be willing to suffer in order to create is one thing; to realize that one's creation necessitates suffering, that suffering is one of the greatest of God's gifts, is almost to reach a mystical solution to the problem of evil.*

—J. W. N. Sullivan

Struggle

SEVERAL years ago I had a discussion with a good friend. During one of the roughest periods of my life, I was facing various struggles, none of which I had chosen. I was talking to my friend about it, not as a way of commiserating, but more for the purpose of clarifying. I will never forget the comment he made. He suggested that maybe it was important to put up with a bad deal temporarily so I would *know* when I had a good deal. Later, he added that sometimes one has to experience pain in order to be able to appreciate the pleasure of life and not take it for granted.

I wish this were not true. And I wish it were not true for me. At this point in my life I often think I should be able to avoid struggle. I figure I have paid my dues. However, I have come to the conclusion, there is only one way that struggle and suffering can be avoided. Simply, it is to stop trying. And giving up is not an option for me.

Even the most successful people have experienced great pain and suffering. Those who never face struggle are the ones who never try. To experience success you must simultaneously be willing to risk failure, defeat, and suffering. You can avoid struggle only if you are willing to avoid success. I think my friend was correct. It's an integral part of life. Those who run from or deny struggle may not have to experience the bitter pain of defeat. But they'll also never revel in the absolute joy of success. If you are ready for lukewarm mediocrity, avoidance of struggle is the path. If you're ready for success, don't get discouraged. As Thomas Edison said, it's " . . . another step forward."—JB

---

*I am not discouraged, because every wrong attempt discarded is another step forward.*

—Thomas Edison

Struggle

MANY student athletes become depressed at the conclusion of football season. I experienced it as a teenager and it happens with my children today. Others have described the let-down after a school play, performance or concert. As an adult I have even experienced some minor dips after finishing writing a book. It's a fairly common experience.

William James once said, ". . . need and struggle are what excite us and inspire us. Our hour of triumph is what brings the void . . ." Struggle is good for you. So is suffering. We take a myopic view when trying to avoid it. Take this baby step. In your journal, make an inventory of your life. Try to locate any necessary struggles you have been evading. Perhaps there is something necessary but painful you have been avoiding. Plan a way to face the conflict rather than ignore it. Record your plan of action in writing. Take three small baby steps toward facing your "struggle" in the next three days. By doing so you will far more rapidly experience success.

Remember, it's one kind of struggle to play "chicken" with a tractor trailer truck and lose. That's not what we're describing. Necessary struggles include doing the hard work of becoming responsible. It's making peace with troubled relationships. It's forgiving someone who has hurt you. Or perhaps it's apologizing to those you have hurt. It's working toward a worthwhile goal, even though you have to face adversity along the way. Baby Step your way through adversity. Success awaits you.—JB

---

*We also rejoice in our sufferings, because we know that suffering produces perseverance; and perseverance, character; and character, hope.*
                                        —**Romans 5:3b, 4** NIV

# Failure

FAILURE (fal´yer) n. 1. A myth. A mistake. The condition or fact of not achieving the desired end, resulting in a painful experience. 2. On Thanksgiving Day in 1962 the Packers were coming off an eighteen-game winning streak that extended back into the previous year. They were handed an embarrassing defeat by the Detroit Lions as millions watched on national television, Coach Lombardi realized it was time to go back to the basics. He was determined to learn from this mistake and come back a better team. After an extremely hard week of practice the Packers went on to beat the Rams and have a 13-1-0 season.

Failure exists. But the Lombardi formula doesn't dwell on it. Coach Lombardi said failure was not getting knocked down, but in failing to get up once you had been knocked down. Defeats aren't failures. They're really learning opportunities. Failure occurs only if you give up.

On the journey to success there are roadblocks. As you get closer to your goal, the obstacles actually increase. Coach Lombardi used to say that it was more difficult to stay on top than it was to get there. Thomas Edison described a similar sentiment. When you give up, you fail. The journey to success is a long and arduous one. It's often tempting to give up. If you do, that's failure. As long as you stay in the game, success is possible. You know, a season of 13-1-0 isn't too bad.—VL, Jr.

---

*It's not whether you get knocked down, it's whether you get up.*
—Coach Lombardi

## Failure

IS it a failure to swing the bat? Is it failure to strike out? You've got to swing the bat to hit a home run. Perhaps striking out is batting practice and a home run is the reward.

I played little league and high school baseball. I never went beyond that point. In all honesty I preferred football to baseball and still do. Yet, I enjoy one particular aspect of baseball far more than my favorite sport. Everyone gets a chance at bat. Everyone gets a chance to hit a home run or strike out. It's not just the backfielder who gets to score. Every player does. I like that. I wish it could be incorporated into all sports. If it were, the participants would be better prepared for life. Life is full of strikeouts. In the November 1996 heavyweight championship bout, Evander Holyfield shocked the world by defeating Mike Tyson. After the fight Mike Tyson, no stranger to either failure or success, made some insightful comments to the press. ". . . People lose all the time. We lose fights. We lose family members. But it's the people who come back from those losses who demonstrate character in life . . ."

Most people have heard stories of Hank Aaron and Babe Ruth. The interesting thing is that they are factual. Hank Aaron hit 714 home runs, but he also struck out over 1,264 times. To hit a home run, you have to swing the bat. If you swing the bat, you may strike out. You may strike out many times. That is the way it is in baseball. It is also the way it is in real life. You will strike out. You will make mistakes. You will fail sometimes. Then you'll have a choice to make. You can swing the bat again or you can give up. If you swing the bat again, you may strike out once more or you may hit a home run. But you must risk one to achieve the other. It worked for Hank Aaron and it will work for you. But you have to swing the bat.—JB

---

*Consider every mistake you make as an asset.*

— Paul J. Meyer

### Failure

I'M very proud of my children. Over the years I have tried to teach this particular principle. It is extremely difficult to learn. My goal has been to help them learn it before they get out of high school. In some ways I have been successful, and in others I haven't.

One of my children is a bright young man who has studied the sport of football since the age of five. He's had the honor of working with many excellent coaches over the years. Yet one particular year he ended up with a football coach who should have been doing something other than coaching. He was not only technically weak but had extremely poor interpersonal skills. On several occasions I had to restrain myself to keep from interfering. My inclination was to change teams. But after considering it, I decided it could be a great teaching opportunity. I waited until the inevitable happened.

My son approached me and asked to have a closed-door conversation. He had a defeated look on his face. "You know, Dad, Coach really doesn't know what he's doing, does he?" Rather than try to defend the coach, I agreed. In fact I told my son he probably knew more about football strategy than his coach did. But then I went on to talk to him about the importance of continually swinging the bat. Life is like this. We are given difficult situations. You can put your bat down and quit playing the game. Or you can hang in there and try for a "home run." Eventually, this is what my son did. The coaching did not improve. But the next year my son had a brilliant coach. In fact the best one he ever had. As we look back on it, we both admit that we learned a great deal from that poor coach. My son learned to keep swinging the bat. And I learned to let him.—JB

---

*No, I beat my body and make it my slave so that after I have preached to others, I myself will not be disqualified for the prize.*
—1 Corinthians 9:27 NIV

Failure

THERE is no failure unless you quit trying. If you swing the bat, you can succeed. If you don't swing the bat, then you've lost. As long as you're swinging, you still have a chance. You can learn from mistakes only if you admit and accept them. If you blame others or circumstances, you will never learn. If you are blaming, you are not focused on improving your weaknesses and you'll repeat the same mistakes over again. The same is true in baseball. If you blame the sun glaring in your eyes when you strike out, you won't learn to adjust your swing. And you definitely can't learn to adjust the sun! You have to focus on what you can control.

Mistakes, like strikeouts, are simply a form of corrective feedback. You can avoid them only if *you do something*. So the best strategy is to consider mistakes as part of life and to look at them as swinging the bat. This week take this baby step. In your journal write a new definition for failure. Write a new definition for mistakes. And write a new definition for strikeouts. It will speed you on your way to success.

Remember, you *fail* your way to success. Napoleon Hill often told a story about Thomas Edison that has become famous. Edison told Hill he hadn't ever failed in an experiment to invent the light bulb. He said he knew over a thousand ways how *not* to invent it. Thomas Edison kept swinging the bat and changed the world. So can you. It might be helpful to read this chapter again. And again. And again. Many people in psychotherapy are in trouble because of problems related in some way to this baby step. Twenty-four hours ago I sat with a young couple in a session. They're both attractive, intelligent and reasonably well-off financially. So why are they in therapy? Each has experienced failure in previous relationships and as a result, is scared to commit to this one. I listened to them at some length and slowly began my response. "If Thomas Edison had thought like you, we'd be sitting here in candlelight . . ."—JB

---

*Failure is success if we learn from it.*

—Malcolm S. Forbes

# Perseverance

PERSEVERANCE (pur´se-vir´ens) n. 1. The holding to a course of action, belief, or purpose, without giving way. 2. Coach Lombardi was denied his goal of being a head coach for many years. He saw assistant coaches with equal or less ability get the jobs he wanted, which couldn't have been easy for him. He could have settled for the life of an assistant coach, but he refused. He persevered. Every day, as an assistant coach at West Point and with the New York Giants, he sought to be the best assistant coach he could be. In the end his perseverance was rewarded, and he made the most of his opportunity in Green Bay.

Perseverance, the ability to "hang on" just a bit longer, is the single greatest determinant of your success. Woody Allen said it this way, "80% of life is showing up." Sounds simple doesn't it? And in a way it is. The only thing being asked of you is that you show up today—this hour, this moment. The past has no hold on you. That's why it's called "the past." And the future? Most of the things you're worried about aren't going to happen—at least not the way you anticipate. So bring your focus, your energy, and your talents to this day. Persevere this day. Then get some sleep and do it again tomorrow.

I can't emphasize too strongly how important perseverance is to your happiness and success. Other qualities mentioned in this book have more pizzazz and many may be tempted to go straight to them as the means to success. But make no mistake. Without perseverance you will never accomplish your goals. Ask any successful person. It's a very important baby step on the journey to success.—VL, Jr.

---

*This is not easy, this effort, day after day, week after week, to keep them up, but it is essential.*

—Coach Lombardi

## Perseverance

THE term perseverance originates from Latin. Its original meaning was that of being very serious. Therefore, a person who perseveres could be described as very serious. That agrees with this book's definition of perseverance. Persistence has a slightly different meaning. Persistence means dogged tenacity. Perseverance is similar to the concept of endurance in the pursuit of a goal. It involves continuous strength and patience in dealing with something arduous. Struggle and difficulty do not intimidate people who have perseverance.

This is one characteristic upon which we all agree. The defining difference between successful people and those who are unsuccessful is not intelligence. It's not "who they know." The true difference is perseverance. Success, victory, and riches yield to the individual who is willing to persevere. One of the biggest obstacles to this, however, is that most people give up so easily. The masses are cynical and feel entitled to success without effort. To make matters worse, they defy anyone who disagrees with them. It's easy to give in and become like everyone else. But if you do, you'll never succeed.

Calvin Coolidge explains it very well. "Your ability to face setbacks and disappointment without giving up will be the measure of your ability to succeed." In the final analysis most philosophers agree you can never simply fail. However, you can give up trying. We suggest you try both persistence and perseverance. Develop the dogged tenacity of persistence and the endurance of perseverance. Both are necessary for long-term success to occur. Tenacity can get you jump-started in the short term. Perseverance can help you in the long haul.

------

*Success seems to be largely a matter of hanging on after others have let go.*

—William Feather

## Perseverance

I can think of one very personal and emotional example about how this particular principle applies. I spent twenty-two months of combat in Vietnam. I feel very strongly about what happened there. I was proud to be there at the time and looking back on it many years later, proud I went. But I must also admit that North Vietnam won the war. They won it due to their willingness to persevere. South Vietnamese and US troops won virtually every major battle of the war. Yet we lost the struggle of perseverance. As a result, we lost the war. The North Vietnamese and Viet Cong had a different mindset. They didn't have the typical one-year-in-and-out rotation. They were fighting for their way of life. They had an investment in the community and the country. They weren't going anywhere. As a result, they were willing to persevere.

Some politicians define this concept as a "war of attrition." I call it a "war of perseverance." Those who persevere win. Everyone else loses. William Feathers said, "Success seems to be largely a matter of hanging on after others have let go." It was that way in Vietnam and it will be that way with your own success.

Years later, it's far easier to analyze. Our goals weren't clear for the Vietnam War. In fact, they conflicted with many people's values and belief systems. MacNamara's plans and strategies worked in industry but were futile in the jungles of Vietnam. It wasn't even clear who was in charge. For some it was the State Department. For others it was the Department of Defense. But most of all, we failed by not understanding the nature of Vietnamese culture or the commitment of a nation defending their homeland. The North Vietnamese were fighting for their freedom. Americans were fighting so they could leave in a year. There's a big difference. It's in perseverance.—JB

---

*Success seems to be connected with action. Successful men keep moving. They make mistakes, but they don't quit.*
                                                    —Conrad Hilton

Perseverance

THOMAS Edison said, "Many of life's failures are men who did not realize how close they were to success when they gave up." The truth is that all successful people fail. They just keep on trying. Thomas Edison did. So can you. Evaluate your life. If you are not as successful as you want to be, perhaps it is because you haven't failed enough.

A friend and I once joked about a formula we both had observed. To become a millionaire, we sarcastically commented, you had to have three ex-wives and three bankruptcies. The comment was made in jest, but it contained an element of truth. Virtually all the highly successful people we knew had experienced both divorce and major financial problems. There is no success without struggle. During such difficult times you may be tempted to quit. Persevere through the pain and you will succeed. Give up and you will only get close.

This week take this baby step. Look at the various times you have tripped up in life. Write about them in your journal. Discuss what you have learned from each struggle. Investigate whether you gave up too soon. Perhaps there is an area in your life where you need to persevere. If there is, make a plan to re-commit. And this time, hang in there. Faith is required to persevere. Find it in the writings of Thomas Edison, William James, the Bible and others. Find it in your own successes as well. Success doesn't require bankruptcy and divorce. But it does demand perseverance. Hang on, and you will succeed.—JB

---

*But you, man of God, flee from all this, and pursue righteousness, godliness, faith, love, endurance and gentleness. Fight the good fight of the faith. Take hold of the eternal life to which you were called when you made your good confession in the presence of many witnesses.*
                                                    —1 Timothy 6:11,12 NIV

# 8

# The Feeling
# of
# Success

*Some men succeed by what they know; some by what they do; a few by what they are.*

—Elbert Hubbard

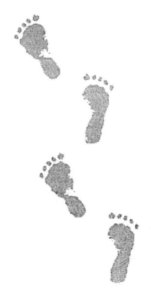

# Will

WILL (will) n. 1. The mental faculty by which one deliberately chooses or decides upon a course of action. 2. In 1962 the Green Bay Packers beat the New York Giants 16-7 for the World Championship. After the season, Coach Lombardi wrote a remarkable letter to his players and equally as remarkable, their wives. Many of them still have the letter. In part, it read, "Character is the perfectly disciplined will and you are men of character. Our greatest glory was not in never falling, but in rising when we fell." To Coach Lombardi, character and will were nearly synonymous. The test of a person's character and will, Lombardi felt, was whether they got up after being repeatedly knocked down.

In speeches I deliver, I often tell people that the difference between great and small people is not so much a lack of strength or education, but a lack of will. It's character, not power, that is our greatest prize. It's character, with its attributes of courage, discipline, loyalty and sacrifice that distinguishes the great from the small. The bottom line for will and character is pride. Too often pride has a negative connotation. It is used in the context of sin. Taken to its extreme, it can be. Excessive pride or conceit does "goeth before the fall." But the pride that comes with having high standards and refusing to compromise those standards is a positive trait. This gives you a strong picture of who you are and what you stand for.

Success can come from the will to use your talents and abilities to the fullest. High achievers are proud of their performance. Whatever the forum, whether it is athletics, business or education, they're prepared to do their best. And nothing can stop them from performing their best. Neither sickness, bad weather, nor the opposition's unethical conduct, can overpower the will of an achiever. In this sense, a disciplined will goeth before success.—VL, Jr.

---

*The difference between a successful person and others is not a lack of strength, not a lack of knowledge, but rather a lack of will.*
—Coach Lombardi

## Will

COACH Lombardi spoke many times of the "perfectly disciplined will." Also, on many occasions, he discussed the will to win. More than any other characteristic, a strong will provides a spirit of determination to your mission. Strength of will comes from deep inquiry into knowing what you believe. It embodies a willingness to sacrifice and work consistently for your beliefs. A strong will creates an energy of its own. *Will* does not take energy. It creates energy.

To have a perfectly-disciplined will you must first know what you believe. Then you can determine what you want. This allows you to passionately commit to a plan to achieve your goals. Knowing what you believe and then determining what you want helps give you the determination to succeed at any cost. Thoreau described it as "living the life you have imagined." Others call it "pursuing your bliss." Coach Lombardi called it the perfectly-disciplined will.

Will is demonstrated most frequently in times of adversity when you defy the odds or your own personal barriers. This was dramatically illustrated many years ago on television. It was the 1980 or 1981 Iron Man Triathlon in Hawaii. One of the women finishers was yards from the finish line, lying on the pavement, exhausted. She swam, biked and ran. Then she had walked, hobbled and stumbled. Finally she crawled, then slithered across the finish line. Tears of exhaustion streamed down her face. She was carried away on a stretcher. It wasn't her strength that prevailed. It was her determination. It was a matter of her perfectly disciplined will. Long after mind and body said, "No!" her will succeeded. The power of your will can do it as well.

---

*Nothing great will ever be achieved without great men, and all men are great only if they are determined to be so.*
                                        —Charles de Gaulle

## Will

THE military is full of opportunities to develop strength of will. There is something about simply surviving the training that develops you. In Marine Corps Officer Candidate School they seem to place particular emphasis on this process. Perhaps more than any other part of my life OCS was a graduate school for strengthening the will. The Marines focused on will, if for no other reason than to ensure you would complete your mission. As a result at times, even if the body screamed "no more," the will caused it to continue.

In Vietnam I found this training to be invaluable. The first time I was wounded, it was rather superficial. Yet there was a great deal of pain and ample bloodshed. Due to the training I had received, I was able to keep my wits about me. Rather than panicking, I was still capable of assisting a fellow combatant in worse shape than I. I ended up carrying a Korean soldier over my shoulder for over three and a half miles along with my weapon, rucksack, and a large radio. Though my body accomplished this, it was controlled by will. And that will was polished through those long days and nights in Marine OCS.

My feat was neither heroic nor incredible. It was simply the will exercising itself over the body. It kept me from panicking from my own problems and helped me assist a friend. There was never a question in my mind that I would do anything else. At that young age I didn't understand the concept. However I practiced it. The same may be true for you. Some of these concerns defy explanation. The need for understanding can sometimes be an obstacle. Don't wait to be convinced. Practice these concepts. Don't understand them. Begin now.—JB

---

*I have brought myself, by long meditation, to the conviction that a human being with a settled purpose must accomplish it, and that nothing can resist a will which will stake even existence upon its fulfillment.*

—Benjamin Disraeli

## Will

A perfectly-disciplined will can keep you going in spite of fatigue, fear, or disbelief. It is often visible in the will to live of many terminally ill medical patients. Countless cases of people who were written off by physicians and given only days to live are telling their story twenty years later. Many who survived, state they accepted the diagnosis—they *were* sick—but not the prognosis or verdict. Doctors can diagnose illness. But only God can determine whether or not you will live.

As a therapist I have worked with many people suffering from cancer and serious heart disease. During the first session I always shock them. The first thing I say is, "Make up your mind right now whether you want to live or die." I spend a great deal of time working with them and their families to build the will to live. But they have to choose life before I go any further. The will to live is that powerful. In these cases, to succeed is to continue living.

The strength of a perfectly-disciplined will is one of the tools you need to succeed. Take this baby step as soon as possible. In your journal write out a twenty-four hour schedule for one week of what you *need* to do. Then follow that schedule for one week. That week do exactly what you need to do. Ignore what you *want* to do. Focus only on what you need to do for one week. Then assess the change that it has made in your life. If it has made you draw closer to success, continue for another week. If it hasn't, reevaluate and make a new schedule.—JB

---

*He will keep you strong to the end.*
                                    —1 Corinthians 1:8a NIV

# Compassion

COMPASSION (kom-pash´on) n. 1. A benevolent kindness and concern for one's fellow man. The deep feeling of sharing the suffering of another. 2. The affection Coach Lombardi felt for his players was manifested in many ways, but none perhaps more graphically than in his sensitivity to bigotry. This was something he had experienced himself. In one of his first speeches to the Packer players he said, "If I ever hear words like 'nigger' or 'dago' or 'kike' or anything like that . . . you're through with me. You can't play for me if you have that kind of prejudice . . . You just have to love your fellow man, and it doesn't matter whether he is black or white." His actions were as strong as his words. During the early sixties the Packers played a preseason game in the deep south. Rather than abide by the Jim Crow laws of the time, Lombardi quartered the team at a nearby military base, where they all suffered equally—without regard to race, color or creed—in non air-conditioned discomfort together.

Too often when we hear the word "love" we associate it with romantic love. So when we are urged to love one another we get a little uncomfortable. Perhaps a better word would be "compassion." Compassionate people care for one another in the knowledge that we are more alike than different. We come from the same source. It is the Source of all life. We all want the same thing. And physically, we're all going to end up the same. Eventually we all die.

The opposite of love is not hate, it's apathy. Apathy is that lukewarm, mealy-mouth feeling—actually it's not feeling. Apathy is non-feeling—you don't care. Perhaps romantic love has a chemical component. Sometimes love just happens. But compassion doesn't just "happen." Like every other attribute mentioned in this book, this love can be nurtured and developed. If I am worthwhile and lovable, then so is everyone else I come in contact with. If they're not lovable and worthwhile, then neither am I.—VL, Jr.

---

*Teamwork is what the Green Bay Packers were all about. They didn't do it for individual glory. They did it because they loved one another.*
—**Coach Lombardi**

## Compassion

MANY years ago I was speaking at an evening banquet. During the meal I overheard a discussion between two men. One commented to the other that his neighbor had been arrested the night before. The second man asked the cause of the arrest. The other responded he wasn't sure. Apparently, he explained, his neighbor had molested his step-daughter. The listener shrugged his shoulders and said, "Nothing surprises me anymore. How 'bout those Braves?"

The difficulty for me as I write this story is that it really did happen. This is not a fictitious illustration to make a point. The conversation occurred just as I have described it. I was so shocked I pulled out several index cards and wrote an account of it at the time. Later, when I made my presentation I referred to the conversation without pointing out the men. I wondered out loud if we were becoming so callous that *nothing* shocked us anymore. We aren't as compassionate as we once were. We don't love as much anymore. I asked if apathy was the new virtue.

Takeo Fugisawa is co-founder and chairman of Honda Motors Company. In a speech many years ago he described Japanese and American management as 95% the same. "However," he added, ". . . it differs in all important aspects . . ." Tom Peters, co-author of *In Search of Excellence*, has described that key 5% difference. He, Fugisawa, and many others have explained that important 5% to be the compassion Japanese management has for their employees. When you lose your compassion, you lose energy for the journey to success. The moment you begin to care again is the moment many tragedies will end. If we collectively care enough about anything, change can occur non-violently. Ghandi proved this. Martin Luther King, Jr. demonstrated it. The dismantling of the Berlin Wall did also. Compassion can move mountains. And it can change modern industry as well.—JB

---

*Love is the only gold.*

—**Alfred Lord Tennyson**

## Compassion

AN unidentified Marine Corps general was interviewed on the Jan. 21, 1992, *ABC News* by reporter Bill Redeker. This was just prior to the beginning of the ground war in the Persian Gulf. Redeker asked the general how he knew the marines would fight. The general answered with words you don't hear from marines very often.

The general said they would fight because they ". . . love. And love is what you use to overcome the feelings of fear, which are natural . . . . What will cause a marine to jump on a hand grenade, killing himself in order to save his fellow marine? Love . . . They fight not because they hate the enemy. They fight because they love their buddies, the Marine Corps, and their country." I have never spoken to a combat veteran who went to war because he hated the enemy. I have never talked to an athlete who said he wanted to win the game because he hated the opponent. Coach Lombardi is correct, as is the Marine Corps general. The basis of all motivation is love. It's something we have lost in our society. Perhaps that is why we have lost some of our motivation as well.

I have noticed a common evolution among several of my friends and mentors who have experienced monetary success. After achieving their career and financial goals, they didn't quit. Instead they began focusing on relationships—especially close ones. Primarily they began to become more compassionate and empathetic. In this way they began to focus on the "mental" aspects of their personal growth. The fascinating result is they grew even more successful. It made them more balanced and healthy. They experienced complete success.—JB

---

*Above all, love each other deeply, because love covers over a multitude of sins.*

—1 Peter 4:8 NIV

## Compassion

ONE of the handouts I use in my seminars starts with the following question, "Why do customers or clients quit?" According to a *US News & World Report* survey, they quit for the following reasons: 1% die; 3% move away; 5% form other friendships; 9% quit for competitive reasons; 14% quit because of dissatisfaction. An incredible 68% quit because of an attitude of indifference by some company employee.

I postulated an "indifference quotient" as a tongue-in-cheek way of predicting success. I suggest the IQ that really matters is not intelligence quotient, but the indifference quotient. Intelligence is important. However I really believe indifference is the defining characteristic. If you don't care and don't love you'll never experience complete success. You'll nibble around its edges. You'll test it. However, you won't taste its sweet nectar.

Take this baby step today. Examine your own indifference ratio. Investigate whether you have joined the ranks of those who "are not surprised anymore." Investigate whether you have quit caring. Then go back to Lombardi's basic principle. Love is the basis of all motivation. Do you want to be successful? Love. Remember, love is not always easy. Sometimes it's frightening. It can be quite painful because the only people who can truly hurt you are those you love. However it's worth it. Compassion is not romantic love. It has nothing to do with sex, fireworks, bells, or whistles. "Dare to care," is the way one person put it. It's good advice.

---

*To love abundantly is to live abundantly, and to love forever is to live forever.*

—Henry Drummond

# Passion

PASSION (pash´en) n. 1. Powerful emotion or boundless enthusiasm. 2. Coach Lombardi was once described by a friend as having the "zeal of a missionary." Lombardi's enthusiasm wasn't reserved just for next Sunday's game. It could be dinner at a nice restaurant, Christmas, or a game of golf. Lombardi's enthusiasm was infectious. People around him couldn't help but be caught up in his passion for life.

In my profession as a speaker, passion is an over-used word. We are told that to succeed we must feel passionate about speaking. No we don't. Speakers can succeed without feeling passionate about their work— and so can you. But in my case, passion helps. Passion and enthusiasm fire the seeds of greatness. Enthusiasm is like an ocean tide. There's a certain inevitability about it. Passion sweeps obstacles away. Some people are enthusiastic by nature. Most of us aren't. I'm not. For those who aren't, passion must be "stoked." Every day we've got to lay on some kindling, strike a match, and fan the flame of passion and enthusiasm.

A popular bit of self-help advice is, "Fake it till you make it." In this one instance the statement has worth. Faking enthusiasm is all right—because it is infectious. Fake it awhile and you will become caught up in it yourself. Try this. Every morning before you begin your day, make a commitment that you will take on your day's events with enthusiasm. I promise you, as the day proceeds, you and those around you will get caught up in this enthusiasm. Before long, what has been faked will be genuine, and you will see the results that comes from real passion. You won't have to fake it any longer.—VL, Jr.

---

*He (Coach Lombardi) taught me that you must have a flaming desire to win. It's got to dominate all your waking hours. It can't ever wane.*
—**Bart Starr,** Quarterback Green Bay Packers, Football Hall of Fame 1977

## Passion

WHEN my children talk about being bored, I tell them they need to find something they feel passionate about. We've often had discussions about this over the years. After a time they quit talking about being bored. Maybe they're tired of hearing the lecture or, hopefully, they have found a passion.

As a society we suffer from terminal boredom. It's not just our children. As a population we have grown so addicted to passive entertainment that we have begun to think that we are entitled to it. We are exposed to extremely entertaining television, videos, computer games, and the internet. It's all wonderful, but it reinforces passive entertainment. Such passivity squelches internal passion.

Passion and passivity come from the same root word. They both originate from the Latin root *pati* meaning "to suffer." In modern usage, they're actually ways of reacting to suffering. You can become passive and depressed. Or you can grow passionate and be filled with boundless enthusiasm. It all depends on the way you respond. Passion is the opposite of passivity. For you, passion may be a thing of the past. You can learn to feel it again. The seeds of passion are found in action. Movement can change passivity to passion. By directing your passion to a worthwhile goal you will achieve whatever it is you set out to do. But you must act. Take action today. You will be on your way to success. Action can lead to passion. While passion and passivity come from the same Latin root, they are polar opposites. They are two different ways of responding to difficulty. Use action to become fueled by passion. Act immediately!—JB

---

*Success is not the key to happiness. Happiness is the key to success. If you love what you are doing, you will be successful.*
                                                        —Herman Cain

## Passion

I have always been fascinated with people who focus on outward appearances. I have met many people over the years who dress impeccably to detract from less attractive emotional qualities. One man I saw for personal coaching fit this description. His emphasis was completely on the external. He wore a three-piece pin-stripe suit directly out of a dress-for-success book. He had a custom tailored monogrammed shirt that he bragged cost well over $200. He drove an extremely expensive car and made a point of flashing his designer key case. His focus was external. But it was a masquerade. Passion can only be found internally.

Sometimes it's difficult for me to help people due to my personal aversion to masquerades. This was one of those cases. I agreed to see the man for three sessions, simply because the company owner was a personal friend. I figured if this man could take what I had to say for three sessions, I'd be wrong about my assessment. I didn't waste any time and got right to the point.

From the first, it was obvious he had many of the necessary qualities to be successful in sales. However, the one component he was missing was passion. Rather than getting "touchy-feely" psychotherapy, he quickly realized I was there to help him create change. Thankfully, we ended up on the same "team." Together we investigated his loss of passion and developed a strategy for rebuilding it. After several weeks his emphasis on externals began to change as the internal passion began to compensate. Within months his performance changed as well. Passion is the true dress for success. Forget about appearances. Focus on passion.—JB

---

*As fire consumes the forest or a flame sets the mountains ablaze, so pursue them with your tempest and terrify them with your storm.*
—**Psalm 83:14, 15** NIV

Passion

PASSION makes people oblivious to "quitting time," schedules, and quotas. When you feel passionate about your work you forget about time and focus on results. Passion makes performers and champions out of each of us. One of my favorite writers is F. Scott Fitzgerald. Several years ago I wrote a book about Scott and his wife, Zelda, entitled *The Zelda Complex*. During that time it was fascinating to psychologically investigate the life of this gifted artist. Fitzgerald said, " . . . France was a land, England was a people. But Americans, still having about it that quantity of the ideal was harder to utter. It was the graves of Shiloh. It was tired, drawn faces of it's great men. It was the country of boys dying in the Argonne for a phrase that was empty before their bodies withered. It was the willingness of the heart."

Fitzgerald was commenting on the fact that passion was what made America great. Dwight Eisenhower said the same thing, perhaps far less poetically. He said, ". . . to change Americans, you must change their heart." It can only be done with passion. The results of passion can be found in the history of American presidential races. It can be found in the history of America's great corporate leaders. It can be found in the results of your own journey to success. Reintroduce passion in your life. Success will follow you.

Take this baby step today. Begin to exercise passion. Recall a time in your life when you felt intense enthusiasm about something. Visualize that time. Remember it in minute detail. See, hear, taste, touch, smell, and experience that moment. Write about it in your journal. Then become that person again. Walk, talk, breathe, stand, and feel identically to that very moment. Capture it. Make it yours. And practice it perfectly. You will soon become it again.—JB

---

*Success is having a flair for the thing that you are doing; knowing that is not enough, that you have got to have hard work and a certain sense of purpose.*

—Margaret Thatcher

# Motivation

MOTIVATION (mo´ti-va´shun) n. 1. The act or process of providing an incentive to stimulate action. 2. Ask any of Coach Lombardi's players and they will tell you he was a great motivator. Probe a little deeper and you will discover that different aspects of the coach's personality worked for different players. Some were motivated by his speeches. Others were motivated by the desire to avoid his biting criticism. Still others were motivated by a wish not to disappoint their coach with a poor effort. Some of the more perceptive players will tell you that Lombardi didn't motivate them. He simply created an environment within which they could motivate themselves.

One of the greatest motivational speeches ever made is found in Shakespeare's *Henry V*. Except in limited situations, speeches don't motivate. But this one is instructive in terms of motivating ourselves and others. The year is 1415 and the English and French are about to meet in battle. The English are outnumbered five to one and they are tired and discouraged. The French, on the other hand, are rested and eager. Listen to Henry as he rallies his troops and scoffs at a general who wishes for reinforcements.

"If we are marked to die, we are enough to do our country loss." (If we're going to lose, we've enough men to lose.) Henry continues, ". . . if to live, the fewer men, the greater share of honor." (Henry is confident of victory and doesn't want to share it with anyone else.) The first point is this. Right now, you have the resources to succeed.

Henry continues, "He that lives this day and comes safe home will stand tiptoe when this day is named . . . And gentlemen in England now abed shall think themselves accursed they were not here." The second point is, your goal is worthy of you. The king concludes, "For he today that sheds his blood with me shall be my brother." Finally, you, and those closest to you, are in this together. Henry then asks the general if he still needs reinforcements. The general replies, "God's will! my liege, would that you and I alone, without more help, could fight this royal battle." The English won.—VL, Jr.

---

*Some need a whip and others a pat on the back and others are better off when they are ignored.*

—Coach Lombardi

## Motivation

PASSION directed toward a worthy goal and channeled appropriately becomes motivation. This motivation fuels and propels you further toward your goal. Motivation comes from the Latin word *Motus* which means "motion." To be motivated is to be moving toward your goal.

Motivation is a misused and abused concept. True motivation is not something someone else gives you. It's something you give yourself. It arrives in its most pure and powerful form as a result of doing all the *babysteps* up to this point. If you have practiced them you will be highly motivated. Authentic motivation is not a pep rally or a fiery speech. Fiery sermons and rousing pep rallies are good for inspiration. But they do not result in motivation. Motivation is an internal concept. It gives you energy. And it actually results from moving toward your goal. It is *motion* and it comes from within, or it doesn't come at all.

Other people can help you find motivation within yourself. But they can't give it to you. There are a lot of things that help. But they can't *provide* it either. You can be inspired, threatened, begged, cajoled, or lied to. Those things can't inject you with motivation. They can "pump you" temporarily. But that's their limit. The secret is this. Motivation is the result of *practicing* these skills repetitively. Do so and you will be motivated beyond belief. And it will come from within. Remember, a "pep rally" may help temporarily. There's nothing wrong with them. They're just not the solution to the long-term problem of motivation. If a motivational speech can inspire you for the short term, that's great. When you internalize motivation however, you are far better off. Internalized motivation begins when you're "in motion" toward a worthwhile goal you have chosen.

---

*Success is not the result of spontaneous combustion. You must set yourself on fire.*

—Reggie Leach

## Motivation

I have told the story on many occasions of a Marine Corps drill sergeant I met when I was in Officer's Candidate School. His one complaint of my performance was that I was not highly motivated. Though I received high marks in every other regard, my motivation scores were always low. Finally in an opportune moment I asked him what he meant by motivation. He responded by saying, ". . . you know. . . motivation . . . the yelling and the screaming."

On another occasion I was speaking to a group at a sales meeting. One of the participants came over to me during the break and told me that I wasn't motivational. I asked him what he meant by that. He explained, ". . . you don't yell . . ." Motivation—in spite of the meeting participant or the drill sergeant—is not yelling. Yet it's easy to confuse these concepts.

Motivation is a scientifically valid and legitimate concept. The way it's distorted today makes it a miracle the concept has any legitimacy whatever. Yet, it's a highly valuable quality. To obtain true motivation, begin moving toward your goal. Use the energy that motion provides to propel yourself even more quickly. If periodic yelling and screaming helps, go for it. But don't mistake a pep rally for motivation. They are two different things. As you progress toward your goal you will feel it. When you do, you may want to shout. But it won't come from your throat. It will originate in your body center. It will feel warm, like a simmering flame that slowly spreads outward in all directions. It's the fire of *motis*. This is the source of authentic motivation. And it's the only kind that's lasting.—JB

---

*Many persons have a wrong idea of what constitutes true happiness. It is not attained through self-gratification but through fidelity to a worthy purpose.*

—Helen Keller

## Motivation

I was riding in a jeep with three other Marines during the Vietnam War. We were headed down a one-lane dirt road in what we thought was friendly territory. As we began to cross a bridge across a rice paddy dike, the sound of mortars exploding at the other end of the dike grabbed our attention. The mortar shells were dropping closer and closer to our jeep. There was not room on the dike to turn around. Since there was nowhere to hide we jumped out of the jeep without discussion. Each of us grabbed a corner. We literally picked the jeep up, turned it around, and sped away in the other direction.

Several hours later back in a safe location, we were telling our friends what had happened. They didn't believe us and insisted that a jeep would be too heavy for the four of us to pick up. Accepting their challenge, we went out and tried to repeat it. We failed miserably. We tried several times and couldn't budge it. Motivation is an internal source of energy. It's composed of inner desires, urges, energy, and instincts. Occasionally, in response to an external stimulus you can be provoked to do the impossible. When facing death we were strong enough to pick up a jeep. That can happen to anybody. The real feat is to continue being motivated in the absence of extreme circumstances.

People who can maintain their motivational level away from the grandiose are those who continually achieve in a big way. Take this baby step. In your journal, structure a motivational program that you will pursue on a daily basis. If you need someone to yell at you, give me a phone call! If you need someone to shoot at you, however, I suggest you reevaluate. Set up a program that will provide you with energy, enthusiasm, and ongoing emotion toward achieving your goal. That is true motivation and will propel you on your way to success.—JB

---

*Behold, we count them happy which endure.*

—James 5:11

# Accepting Responsibility for Your Success

*Mighty rivers can easily be leaped at their source.*
—Publilius Syrus

# Responsibility

RESPONSIBILITY (ri-spon´si-bil´i-te) n. 1. A duty, obligation, or burden. 2. Coach Lombardi was most demanding of his talented players. He believed that all his players had a responsibility to use their talent to the fullest, and the truly gifted had an extra obligation. Also, it was his responsibility to prod those gifted players to do their best. Nevertheless, Lombardi could excuse physical mistakes, especially if one of his players was matched up against a superior opponent. What Lombardi refused to overlook were mental errors. He insisted that mental errors showed a lack of preparation, something within the individual responsibility of each player.

The other day I was scheduled to fly from Detroit through Chicago to Seattle. When I arrived at the Detroit airport, I discovered my flight was canceled. No problem, said the reservation agent, I could still get on a flight to Chicago that had been delayed. "Just go to the gate and they will give you a seat," she said. I went to the gate only to discover I was on standby. This is quite different from having a confirmed seat. I informed the gate agent of this and he proceeded to put the blame on me! I can abide delayed, even canceled flights. But one thing I will not accept is the refusal to accept accountability, and I so informed the gate attendant.

Who was more irresponsible here? The attendant who refused to take accountability for the misinformation given me by a fellow airline employee? Or me, who, faced with a frustrating situation, chose to vent and take it out on the gate agent? Responsibility can be heavy. But try as we might, we can't avoid it. For what goes around does come around. You can avoid responsibility for a while. But sooner or later you will sit down to a banquet of consequences. And the longer you put off taking responsibility, the more distasteful the banquet.—VL, Jr.

---

*I think a boy with talent has a moral obligation to fulfill it, and I will not relent my own responsibility.*
                                                            —Coach Lombardi

## Responsibility

WE live in a society where it is far more popular to blame than to accept responsibility. From the Bobbitts to the Menendez brothers to Tanya Harding, blame has become a way of life. People blame dysfunctional families, ADD, PMS, and any other alphabet soup they are allowed to use. One of the most fascinating stories of this was the one about a former jockey. He sued the state of California, saying the roads were unsafe for him to drive on while intoxicated. It's unfortunate that this gentleman suffered debilitating injuries from the accident. But the responsibility is not with the people who built the road. It's with the person who chooses to overindulge.

The mantra of the moment is, "It's not my fault," and we hear it all the way from five-year-olds to politicians. Everyone has an excuse, and rarely does anyone want to accept blame. This is unfortunate, because, in reality, taking responsibility is the best way to change. Taking responsibility empowers you. Blaming the past, circumstances, or other does not. Take the responsibility yourself. Only then can you begin to change.

The truth is, whatever you give will be returned to you many times over. You are completely responsible for your life. No one else is. There are, in fact, a few exceptions to this—but *only* a few. You will always be fully compensated for whatever you do. As the title of Dr. Robert Schuller's latest book says, *"If it's going to be, it's up to me."* This is difficult to accept. But the moment you do you're on the fast road to success. It's not easy. It's much easier to blame others. Earl Nightingale used to say we are all self-made. But only successful people are willing to admit it. No one ever says, "I'm a self-made derelict." Somehow we take responsibility only for our successes. Try taking responsibility for your defeats as well. Then you can begin changing them.

---

*Man must cease attributing his problems to his environment, and learn again to exercise his will—his personal responsibility in the realm of faith and morals.*

—**Albert Schweitzer**

## Responsibility

IT'S easy to accept responsibility for your successes or victories. "If it is to be, it's up to me." Sure. If you win, it's easy to accept that. However, it's far more difficult when you are trying to explain away a problem. Miraculously, blame works for a lot of people. It even works in court. One lady was actually acquitted of murder due to PMS. That sets a dangerous precedent for a lot of husbands. But blame doesn't seem to work with the IRS. I have it on reliable authority that they don't care about PMS!

Factually, the best thing you can do is to accept responsibility. No excuse is the best excuse. If it is to be, it's up to me. If it is not to be, it's still up to me. Only by accepting responsibility and empowering yourself can you begin to change your life. The math on this baby step really does add up. Any time I blame, I'm giving control to whatever or whoever I'm blaming. If I blame my problems on you, that's the same as saying you control me. If I accept responsibility, I have to blame myself. But at the same time, I maintain control.

Emerson said, ". . . There is a time in every man's education when he arrives at the conviction . . . that though the wide universe is full of good, no kernel of nourishing corn can come to him but through his toil bestowed on that plot of ground which is given to him to till . . ." Let this be that time in your education. Give up on blame today. Success awaits you. But you must till the soil. It is your plot of ground and your work that will produce the "nourishing corn." After all, if it is to be, it's up to you!

---

*Unto whomsoever much is given, of him shall much be required.*
—Luke 12:48

Responsibility

FOR the past twenty years it has been popular to blame criminal behavior on psychological problems. The moment this began was the moment individual responsibility was lost. Not only is it unfortunate, it was a tremendous and tragic turning point for our society.

We may be able to intellectually understand that "Billy" shot his father due to an abusive childhood. Because we understand it, however, does not mean he should be allowed to evade responsibility. As Lillian Smith said, "Freedom is a dreadful word unless accompanied by responsibility. And mankind may disappear from the face of the earth unless the minds of men grow mature." Responsibility goes hand in hand with freedom. The more these two concepts become separate, the more your own freedom will disappear.

Take this baby step today. In your journal write about one example in your life when you have evaded responsibility. Describe an occasion when you rationalized and blamed someone else or circumstances. Consider how the results could have changed if you had accepted responsibility and taken an action step, rather than blaming. Remember this extremely important concept. The moment you accept responsibility you empower yourself. When you blame, you avoid responsibility, but you weaken yourself and simultaneously strengthen whatever you blame. If it is to be, it's up to me. That will never change.

---

*As human beings, we are endowed with freedom of choice, and we cannot shuffle off our responsibility upon the shoulders of God or nature. We must shoulder it ourselves. It is up to us.*

                                                        —Arnold J. Toynbee

# Past

PAST (past) n. 1. The time before the present; no longer current; over and done with; existing in an earlier time. 2. Coach Lombardi studied the past but he lived in the present. He understood that in the world of sports dwelling in the past was a prescription for defeat. Lombardi coached five NFL championship teams. He knew that if a championship team focused on last year's season, they wouldn't remain champions for long. Therefore, at the beginning of each season he resisted all suggestions that the Packers would be "defending" last year's championship. Rather, he insisted each season represented a new and separate challenge. He reminded his players that *this* team would have to make its own mark. And each player had to earn his position again, regardless of what he had accomplished in years past.

Tolstoy, the great Russian writer, is credited with the story of an emperor who felt he could govern with wisdom if he had the answers to three questions. "When is the best time to do each thing? Who are the most important people to work with? What is the most important thing to do at all times?" Aren't those great questions? Would you agree with the emperor that if you had the answers to those questions you could be wise and successful? The story goes on to say that the emperor was dissatisfied with the answers given him by his advisors so he determined to consult with a hermit who lived in his empire. Many adventures later, the emperor answered his own questions, although the hermit had to point this out to him.

The answers? There is only one important time, and it is now. The most important person is the person you are with right now. The most important thing to do is whatever you are doing now—the present. There's a reason why it's called the present—it's a gift. This is sound psychologically and theologically. Meister Eckart, a great spiritual teacher from the 16th century wrote, "When God finds you ready, no attention is paid to what you were, God accepts you for who you are . . ."—VL, Jr.

---

*I've never been a losing coach, and I don't intend to start here . . . I'm going to find thirty-six men who have the pride to make any sacrifice to win. There are such men. If they're not here, I'll get them. If you are not one, if you don't want to play, you might as well leave right now.*
—Coach Lombardi

Past
---

YOU are not your past, though it is the excuse most people use when they are attempting to evade responsibility. People say it in therapy regularly. "I can't do that. I had a bad childhood." If Coach Lombardi had blamed the past, we all know what would have happened to the Green Bay Packers. They were perennial losers when he went to Green Bay. But he didn't let their dismal past stop him.

In 1959 the forty–six–year–old Vince Lombardi became the Packers' head coach. Over the next decade that group of "cellar dwellers" won five world championships. Yet no one could have ever predicted it by looking at their past. Lombardi understood the past, but he didn't blame it. He didn't justify losses by discussing what he inherited as head coach. He realized this team was not the past. The past does not equal the present. The present does not determine the future. You can allow it to. Certainly you are influenced by your past, just as we all are. You are also influenced by the size of your nose. But you're not controlled by your nose unless you choose to be. It is totally up to you. Decide today not to let your negative past control you.

You are not your past. You are not your parents. You're not what your ex–spouse or your ex–employer thought you were. And you're definitely not the mistakes you made ten years ago. Don't blame the past. Learn from it. You will be far more effective on your journey to success. One of the keys all successful people practice is this. *Learn from the past. Live in the present. Look to the future.* Try that as your motto. The present is where you focus. Work on your goals in the present. The future and the past will take care of themselves.

---

*There is the greatest practical benefit in making a few failures early in life.*

—**Thomas Henry Huxley**

## Past

NOT only are you not your past, you are not any of the labels that people place on you. You are not your skin color, hair color, or waist size. You are not your height, your weight or your spouse's accomplishments. You are also not the lack of any of these things.

There are people who blame virtually anything. One man visiting me in therapy blamed his first name for his troubles. I told him to change it. Another blamed his mother. I told him his mother was a biological accident. She had donated an egg and a man had donated sperm. As a result he was the biological reality. I told him to adopt another mom if the one who had given birth to him acted merely as an egg donor.

The strangest excuse I ever heard was from someone who blamed their problems on the fact that he had been raised a Baptist. Perhaps I missed his point. I don't care if you, like the fictitious Tarzan, were raised by apes. You still are not your past. The past is over. You are here now. They are two totally different things, unless you choose to remain your past. I don't advise it. I have a better suggestion. Focus instead on creating your future. Rather than dwell on your past, focus on how you want to change your life. Instead of emphasizing the mistakes of yesterday, visualize everything right about tomorrow. Do this. And you will be well on the journey to success. There will be slips along the way. Occasionally thoughts about the past will sidetrack you. Tell those thoughts to leave you alone. They aren't your friends. Replace those thoughts with positive self-talk and healthy visualization. It will keep you on track during your journey.—JB

---

*Forgetting those things which are behind, and reaching forth unto those things which are before, I press toward the mark.*
                                        **—Philippians 3:13b-14a**

Past

MANY people with terrible pasts suffered some of the worst imaginable kinds of abuse. They choose never to let it affect them at all. In fact, they usually don't talk about it. Sometimes it's shocking to discover how difficult some people had it in their earlier years. These people are not in denial. They simply refuse to let something beyond their influence control them. They don't deny the past, but they place it right where it belongs. They put it *in* the past. Most of us don't do that. Instead we empower the past. But the moment you do so, you lose control of your life.

Look at your own past. Perhaps there is something you have to say good–bye to. With a friend, discuss the people, events or circumstances you still hold resentments against. If talking doesn't help, enter psychotherapy if necessary. Go to a seminar. Buy a book. Do what you have to do. But get over it. Incidentally, if anybody—especially a therapist—blames your past, quickly get away from him. He may be well-intentioned, but it doesn't help. Don't blame the past. Use it to help you *understand* the present. Then move on. Sympathy sometimes feels good, but it doesn't help you create change. Whatever you have suffered can be used to strengthen you and help others. Or, it can be an opportunity for self pity.

Take this baby step today. Turn the past into something positive. Help yourself. Then help others. If it helps to talk to your "inner child" feel free to do so. If it helps to kick your "inner child" out from where he or she is hiding, do that. If you're simply tired of excuses then focus on the "you" of the present and work toward the future. Make a list of resentments or grudges in your journal. Discuss the list with an intelligent, reliable friend. Write letters to the people on your list—don't send them, just write them. Discuss your feelings in your letters. Cry if you need to. Beat up a pillow if it will make you feel better. Yell, scream, and get nauseous if that's what it takes. Afterwards, if you feel like you've let go, great! It you're still angry about the past, get professional help. In all seriousness, nothing will destroy your life more quickly than problems with the past.

---

*It is not I that belongs to the past, but the past that belongs to me.*
—Mary Antin

# Creativity

CREATIVITY (kre-a'tiv-i-ti) n. 1. Characterized by originality and expressiveness; imaginative. 2. Anyone who could design an offense as successful as that of the Packers' had to be creative. But Vince Lombardi's creativity seemed to move to a higher plane. Most offensive football coaches seek to find a weakness in the opposing defense that can be exploited. Conversely, many defenses are drawn to cover up a weakness. Lombardi approached offensive football differently. His thinking was that if the Packers could defeat their opponents at their strongest point they would become demoralized. The rest would be easy.

It is a misconception that some of us are creative and the rest are not. Creativity, like so many of the qualities found in this book, can be accessed and nurtured. One technique is to use "random access." You begin by having a clear objective in mind. Next, you pick up a newspaper or magazine and with your eyes closed, point to a word. Then begin to brainstorm on what this randomly chosen word might mean to your objective. As an example. A rural bank was striving to invent a new advertising campaign. The word they randomly chose was, "chicken." They brainstormed, "feathers," "egg," "crossing the street." Finally someone thought of "nest egg." That was it! The bank's ad campaign featured a nest egg that the bank could help build for their customers' future.

Another way to access your creativity is through a process called, "contradictory message." I've used this method in my speaking business. When trying to think of the benefits a client would derive from hiring me, I first imagine all the advantages they would miss if they didn't. I know they would miss some excellent information complemented by interesting stories, delivered in an impactual, inspiring manner. I then turn these negatives into the positive benefits they would experience by hiring me. Using these techniques, as well as others, you can awaken the spark of creativity that resides in everyone.—VL, Jr.

---

*In all my years of coaching, I have never been successful using somebody else's play . . . It makes you feel that you are losing whatever creativity you have had.*

—Coach Lombardi

Creativity

KEENAN Brewster said, "There is a correlation between creativity and the screwball, so we must suffer the screwball gladly . . ." Over the years these two populations have been frequently confused. Creative geniuses such as Einstein, Marconi, and Thomas Edison were called far worse than screwballs. And the real screwballs have rationalized their bizarreness by claiming to be creative—or even worse—calling their trash art!

The kind of creativity to seek after is that which is productive, pragmatic and functional. It's creativity with an end in mind. It is not creativity as an end in itself. Creativity for its own sake is in a different category. What we are discussing here is goal-oriented. It is creativity with a purpose.

Every leap forward in life began as an idea. Before it became a sketch or even a diagram it was pure thought in some wonderful human mind. Then it was acted upon. Whether in art or technology, creativity begins with this first step. The functionally creative mind blends logic with artistic qualities and invents something productive. All successful people I have known have this attribute. They blend what is commonly referred to as the left and right side of the brain and blend that which is both artistic and useful. You can have this quality as well. But you have to practice it. If this process is a problem for you, read literature on creativity. Many community colleges offer creative thinking courses through their continuing education department. Other people offer seminars or audio and video tapes on the subject. Seek these opportunities. Learning creativity will help you on your journey to success.

---

*It is the function of creative men to perceive the relations between thoughts, or things, or forms of expression that may seem utterly different, and to be able to combine them into some new forms—the power to connect the seemingly unconnected.*

—William Plomer

Creativity

CREATIVITY is no respecter of age. This is one way that it is different from some of the other principles in this book. Much of success has to do with age, because with added years comes added opportunity to invest hours. While creativity can result from hours invested, it can also result from a flash of insight.

This flashing insight can occur at any age. I have talked to many people who had a creative thought and acted on it with tremendous success. Though this idea may be followed by hours or even years of activity to bring it to fulfillment, it began only as an idea. In some instances it was a childhood dream or fantasy that was later acted upon. This could have occurred in the person's youth. Einstein himself was a tremendous dreamer. As a young man he dreamed about riding on a beam of light to the end of the universe. As a result of these musings he discovered the theory of relativity. Einstein said that imagination was more important than knowledge. He certainly should have known.

Intelligence and creativity are quite different. Intelligence is knowledge acquired through learning. Creativity is the ability to apply intelligence in some inventive manner. Intelligence will tell you to conform—to color inside the lines. Creativity will goad you into coloring outside the lines and manifest itself in a Picasso–like work of art. Practice creativity regularly.

---

*Man unites himself with the world in the process of creation.*
—Erich Fromm

Creativity

CREATIVE people are often looked on as being one-track minded. Nothing could be further from the truth. Einstein was a yachtsman, violinist, astronomer, mathematician, teacher, artist, physicist and scientist. Look at the truly productive creative individual and you will find the same thing. They are active. They are diverse. Many are accomplished athletes. Virtually all are extremely active and make walking a hobby.

It is this diversity of mental and physical effort that makes them great. Whether it's stimulating *both sides of the brain* or just balancing things out is irrelevant. There are many suggestions as to why this is true. Some say it's the increased oxygenation to the brain. Others suggest it's the biochemical changes exercise causes to the brain. Still others describe it as a result of stimulation to the central nervous system through a combination of events. Regardless, the fact is that creativity is more likely to be found in an active diversified mind than in a more restricted, passive and sedentary one.

Take this baby step today. Practice creativity in one area of your life. Follow this formula: A) Write the problem or idea on a piece of paper. B) Brainstorm different ideas for solving the problem. C) After sixty minutes of brainstorming walk away from the problem. Get some exercise or go for a walk. D) Then relax and approach the problem for another sixty minutes and see what results you generate. E) If nothing pops out don't worry about it. It will later. Follow this formula. It will help you become more creative and more successful. Remember to apply the ideas you come up with.

Creativity is helpful only if you act on it. The idea may, and often does, occur "like a thief in the night." You may awaken at 3:00 a.m. and feel you have been struck by lightning. The answer may hit you while you are showering or walking or at some other unexpected time. But it will always be a result of the brainstorming and thinking you did earlier. To be great, create.

---

*In the beginning God created the heaven and the earth . . . and God saw that it was good.*

—Genesis 1:1 & 10b

# Innovation

INNOVATION (in´u-va´shun) n. 1. That which is newly introduced; creative change. 2. Coach Lombardi reasoned that if he could defeat the best men on the opposing team, he would destroy their morale and win the game. To this end he devised innovative strategies to neutralize star players such as Gino Marchetti, Sam Huff, and Night Train Lane. These strategies did not change the Packers' game plan. However, Coach Lombardi constantly kept in mind the unique strengths of his opponent. Innovation was the way he adjusted to those strengths.

Coach Lombardi modeled all the principles we discuss in this book. After all, this is his philosophy. We're simply the writers. The principles created a strong foundation. Not much was left to chance. The Packers were so well prepared, physically, mentally, and emotionally, that winning was inevitable. But just as in life, in spite of all his preparation, there were times when his plans fell through. When they did Coach Lombardi innovated.

When he coached high school basketball without playing the game himself, innovation was necessary. (Incidentally, he won a state championship.) A similar thing happened with football. Other coaches began adapting philosophies almost identical to Coach Lombardi's. As a result, their teams played at a higher level. As this occurred, Lombardi innovated more to compensate and create a greater competitive advantage. With each game he didn't rewrite his play book, or create trick plays. He innovated in ways to strengthen the game plan and weaken that of his opponent's. Innovation is a strength. It's one of fifty-two strategies Coach Lombardi modeled. You practice it as well. It's a baby step on the path to success.—VL, Jr.

---

*He (Coach Lombardi) was an innovator, willing to experiment to make his team more effective.*
—**Merv Hyman,** Sports writer for Englewood Press, home of St. Cecilia High

Innovation

ONE of the great innovators of all time was Pablo Picasso. Apparently Picasso was sitting in a Paris restaurant one afternoon with F. Scott Fitzgerald, Gertrude Stein, and Ernest Hemingway. They were minding their own business while eating lunch.

A lady approached Picasso and begged him to draw something on her napkin. After protesting several times, he finally gave in to the woman's demands. He scribbled something on the paper, handed it back to her, and suggested his fee for the drawing was $50,000 dollars. ". . . Maestro," she protested with tears in her eyes, "It only took you five minutes!" After pausing for a moment Picasso made eye contact with her and responded, *"No you don't understand. It's taken me my entire life."*

This happens with many talented people. They can become so skilled at what they do they make it look easy. It's at this point they can truly improvise and innovate. What looks spontaneous to others is actually the result of years of training, hard work, and long hours of study. This woman missed the point. She wasn't paying for five minutes of Picasso's time. She was paying for his mastery. Because of his mastery he could produce a beautiful sketch on her napkin in five minutes and make it look easy. With the same mastery you can innovate too. Learn to innovate and you will expedite your success. Then apply that innovation to pursuing your own goals. Realize such mastery takes years. What looks like innovation is actually the height of skill. Picasso had it in art. Robin Williams has achieved this status in stand-up comedy. Yehudi Menuin gained similar mastery with his violin. They can all innovate with skill. So can you. Innovation springs from hours of preparation. To innovate better than the next person, prepare more.

---

*The intelligent man is always open to new ideas. In fact, he looks for them.*

—**Proverbs 18:15** LB

## Innovation

MY best friend and partner is Shannon McKnight. We have many differences, but our common interests and goals transcend them. One of those minor differences is in how to organize projects and the general level of "messiness" allowable on a project table. Her idea is that everything needs to stay stacked on a desk "until the work is done." On a book this can mean a period of months. I politely disagree, but it's her ten-foot conference table filled to overflowing with files. Later, I visited her mother's office. There was an identical ten-foot conference table piled with hundreds of files. I asked her mother to explain and she replied, "The work isn't done yet." Very seriously she added, "A messy desk is the sign of a creative mind!" She went on to say that since she was a genealogist her files were rarely complete. That, of course, explained the sheer volume of clutter! Shannon was simply following her mother's example of the way work is done. After all, if you grow up with those expectations, that's the way it's supposed to be.

I had a similar experience in my own life. I returned home from graduate school to attend the funeral of one of my grandparents' friends. I questioned them about why we continued to bury people following the customs of the Old South. According to tradition, the dead body is brought into the home and relatives and neighbors sit up with it for three days and three nights. I was given various explanations. One person suggested it had to do with the Bible. Another explained that it had to do with Irish folklore. A ninety-year-old funeral director later explained his version of the reason. He told me that in the old days people had to stay up with the body to keep rats off. If he's correct, we had built a series of semi-religious traditions and customs based on this functional necessity and believed that was the way it was "supposed" to be.

Perhaps the biggest enemy to innovation is "supposed to" thinking. I respect tradition. I believe it's incredibly important. Unfortunately, we have lost too much of it. Yet it's a mistake to be controlled by it. This is especially true with functional problems. If there is a better way to do something, do it. Turn problems into opportunities. Learn to innovate.—JB

---

*The soul without imagination is what an observatory would be without a telescope.*

—Henry Ward Beecher

## Innovation

FRANK Lloyd Wright was one of the great innovators in our country's history. He said that to be truly good at innovation you must have ". . . a vision of the future and an inclination toward rebellion." Great innovators have a crystal clear futuristic vision of what they want to create. They can not only visualize it, they can also describe it in multi-dimensional detail. The inclination toward rebellion results in their not trusting pat answers. Consequently, they are always looking for a better way.

This small degree of unrest is the embryo of all innovation and improvisation. But it doesn't come easily, by any stretch of the imagination. Skilled people make it look easy. The innovator can do this because he is able to see beyond traditional and conventional thought. He can look at the problem from several different angles and it becomes an opportunity to create. It's an opportunity to find an innovative way to arrive at a solution.

Take this baby step today. In your success journal write about several problems in your life. Decide whether you are tempted to solve them using traditions from your past. Perhaps there is a better way. Don't be blinded by definitions of the past. Innovate. See if you can create a better way. Turn your problem into an opportunity to find an innovative solution. This is what Frank Lloyd Wright meant. The "inclination toward rebellion" is not being disrespectful or disobedient. It's merely the willingness to try new answers to old questions. Give it a shot today. Coach Lombardi did. And the results are history.

---

*Research is to see what everybody else has seen, and to think what nobody else has thought.*

—Albert Szent-Gyögyl

# 10

# Sharing Success

*There are some things we do simply because the doing is a success.*
—Nikki Giovanni

# Teamwork

TEAMWORK (tem´wurk) n. 1. Cooperative effort by the members of a team to achieve a common goal. 2. Coach Lombardi was a religious man. Yet he didn't consider a championship a sign of divine favor. Rather, he considered it the result of a few men working closely together in a spirit of discipline and singleness of purpose. With a singular commitment to excellence they could win, no matter how the odds were stacked against them. Coach Lombardi understood that teams, not individuals, won NFL championships. No matter how individually talented you might be, to play for Vince Lombardi you had to be a good teammate with the qualities of sacrifice, discipline, commitment, trust, and respect.

As a speaker, I have the opportunity to talk with managers from all over the world. I often ask them about the young people joining their companies just out of high school or college. They tell me that young people today possess many outstanding qualities. But the managers also indicate that one thing they are lacking is a sense of teamwork. They tell me that young hires are mainly interested in getting visibility, enhancing their reputation within the company, and being noticed by upper management. This kind of attitude gets attention, but not always positive notice.

This is hardly surprising as teamwork is learned. Our instincts are to ask, "What's in it for me?" Unless you have participated in team sports, served in the military, or had some other opportunity to experience teamwork, it's difficult for many to believe that few people achieve success on a solo basis. This is one reason why I am so pleased to see women's athletics grow popular. Until recently, women did not have the opportunity to experience teamwork through sports. Thankfully, this is changing. But it also saddens me that there is so much attention given to "winning" in sports at the grade school and high school levels. With this emphasis, only the gifted athlete has the opportunity to experience the benefits of team sports. Take the time to learn the fundamentals of teamwork and watch your success soar.—VL, Jr.

---

*Individual commitment to a group effort—that is what makes a team work, a company work, a society work, a civilization work.*
—Coach Lombardi

Teamwork

THE theme of this chapter comes from one of my favorite selections in the Bible. The author of Ecclesiastes says, "Two are better than one; because they have a good reward for their labor. For if they fall, the one will lift up his fellow: but woe to him that is alone when he falleth; for he hath not another to help him up. Again, if two lie together, then they have heat; but how can one be warm alone? And if one prevail against him, two shall withstand him; and a threefold cord is not quickly broken."

Regardless of your religious orientation, the official quote is a very poetic passage. And regardless of your philosophy, it's very clear that it is difficult to succeed alone. Scientists, philosophers, theologians, and professional football coaches all agree on this point. As an example, a team of eleven quarterbacks has never won a football game. In fact they would argue about who's in charge. To be successful a team effort is required.

When Coach Lombardi took over the Green Bay Packers they were a team without stars or respect. When he left the Green Bay Packers, many of the players were household names. Some say the team made the stars. Other people say the stars made the team. There certainly were a large number of All-pros on the Packers when Lombardi left. But most of the same players were there when he arrived. In our opinion, it was the team and coach that made the All-pros and not vice versa. In the case of the Green Bay Packers, two were greater than one. We believe you will find this is true in your life as well.

---

*No employer today is independent of those about him. He cannot succeed alone, no matter how great his ability or capital. Business today is more than ever a question of cooperation.*
                                        —Orison Swett Marden

## Teamwork

THERE are times when two may not be "better" than one, but they definitely are more powerful. The Oklahoma City disaster proved the power that otherwise harmless chemicals can have when blended together and ignited. Fertilizer is a very useful chemical. So is diesel fuel. Blended together with a small ignition device, the two caused incredible pain, suffering, and loss of life.

People can have a similar reaction with each other. Two otherwise very healthy and functional people can get together and produce a toxic reaction. One of the tragic things about this type of relationship is the difficulty these people have in staying away from each other. Individually, the two don't have a great deal of difficulty. However, together they become insane. Two are more powerful than one. In this case the two, individually, are far different from the sum of their parts. This is true in chemistry. It's also true in some relationships.

Hydrogen and oxygen blended together properly create a new substance called water. Water is different from the sum of its parts. Two or more people blended together also create a substance different from the sum of their parts. It's called a team. Or it's called a disaster. The proper combination is very important. Choose your team carefully. Many people don't. Conservative statistics indicate well over 3,000 women and 1,500 men die each year at the hands of their spouses! That's an incredibly large number of toxic relationships. And it's a high price to pay. Fertilizer and diesel fuel are deadly when mixed and ignited. Build your team. But do it carefully.

---

*Two can accomplish more than twice as much as one, for the results can be much better. If one falls, the other pulls him up; but if a man falls when he is alone, he's in trouble. And one standing alone can be attacked and defeated, but two can stand back-to-back and conquer; three is even better, for a triple-braided cord is not easily broken.*
—Ecclesiastes 4:9-10, 12 LB

## Teamwork

ERICH Fromm said, "A person's inability to overcome aloneness leads to insanity." We agree. Isolation will destroy you. This is probably why people find themselves propelled together in spite of the resulting toxic chemistry. We believe in relationships. We believe in friends. We also believe in being very careful about how you choose those friends. If you find yourself reacting "chemically" to another person, it is probably better to back off. It can be tempting, scintillating, and enticing. However that may be an even better reason to stay away. Two are better than one, but not when they produce a toxic reaction.

There is no such thing as a "self-made man." Any successful person will be the first to tell you there are many who helped him along the way. Individual commitment to group effort creates a team. The same principle can work in your own journey toward success. Successful people don't lead isolated lives. They all have mastermind groups, either formally or informally, to help them achieve their goals.

Napoleon Hill's classic *Think and Grow Rich* discusses the concept of "mastermind." The concept pre-dates his book but, to my knowledge, he was one of the first to write about it. Hill described a mastermind group as gathering with frequency to advance one or all toward a goal. The members may not call it a "mastermind" yet it serves the same function. They may gather for the purpose of helping one particular individual. Other times they serve as a mutual support network. Take this baby step today. Two are better than one. It is time for you to become part of a mastermind group. Begin this process by reading or rereading Napoleon Hill's chapters on the subject. Then make a goal to form a mastermind group within the next month. In your success journal write down the steps you can take to organize a group. Then work on it. It's a baby step on the road to success.

---

*There is no such being as a "self-made" person. Those who have truly earned the world's respect and admiration for their outstanding accomplishments are always quick to point out the many helping hands, throughout their life, that helped them reach the pinnacle.*

—Og Mandino

# Service

SERVICE (sur´vis) n. 1. An act of assistance or benefit to another. 2. To Coach Lombardi, serving others made him feel closer to God. As a result, he was active in a variety of community charities. More important than giving money or endorsements was his willingness to take an active part in charities where he could serve others. Lombardi was never so successful that he couldn't help his fellow man.

Coach Lombardi didn't have to "preach" about service. He lived it. It was as much a part of him as breathing. His entire life focus was on improving the spirituality, family, and careers of those whose lives he touched. His priorities of God, family, and the Green Bay Packers were real to him. Obviously, he occasionally erred. But his heart was definitely in the right place. Coaching was nothing more than the way he offered his service to God and his fellow man.

Coach Lombardi believed in the sacrificial nature of individual service and even human existence. The team was far more important than one person's ego. In fact, he was intolerant of individual ego. He had little use for someone whose main purpose was to glorify himself. For Lombardi, the role of an individual was that of service to the team. Coach Lombardi had tremendous drive and energy. He had the unique singular trait of being able to motivate himself and others to thier limits and beyond. His commitment is legendary. He had equal portions of toughness, discipline, and compassion all wrapped in the same package. Paradoxically these qualities could be summed up in this phrase—service to others.—VL, Jr.

---

*For all who make it, there's got to be a selflessness, a sublimation, automatically, of the individual to the whole.*

—**Coach Lombardi**

## Service

TO be truly successful you cannot be self-absorbed. If you want to help yourself, focus on becoming involved in service to others. This is true in individual and organizational growth. The only way to receive anything from others—or life—is to give. Then you will receive. Many people, including Dr. Karl Menninger and Dr. Carl Jung, said the same thing utilizing different concepts. Asked what advice they would give people suffering from depression, each man made similar suggestions. Their wisdom was to find someone even more depressed and help that person. Give and you will receive.

People involved with helping others have a longer life expectancy, fewer health problems, and report themselves as being more at peace. They have less depression, are happier, and have fewer complaints with life in general. Becoming involved in service to others gets the focus off you. You become a giver. The eventual result is you receive far more in return. Learn to do this. When you do, you will be on the road to success.

Coach Lombardi became successful by making those around him successful. He didn't call attention to himself. He didn't have to. He made the team better. And as a result, Coach Lombardi became a household name. Give. And you will receive. At the same time, give to those who'd understand the importance of giving back. There's nothing more rewarding than being in a relationship where the "significant other" gives back. The other may not be able to give the same way you do. But that's not necessary. Don't ask them to be like you. However, do expect them to give. Nothing will empty you like giving to someone who absorbs but doesn't return. Give and you will get. However don't give to an empty shell.

---

*The pleasure we derive from doing favors is partly in the feeling it gives us that we are not altogether worthless.*
                                                    —Eric Hoffer

## Service

KEN Martin is a friend of mine who is the number one carpet salesman in the world. He's very busy and we rarely have the opportunity to speak personally. We have lunch together on the average of once a month. During these discussions we talk about life in general. And I always try to get him to discuss sales and marketing.

Ken's formula is fairly simple. If your phone is not ringing you should be dialing. If there are no incoming calls make outgoing ones. If not enough business is coming in, go find it. If you do that enough, your phone will begin ringing constantly, and you won't have to worry about outgoing phone calls. The second part to his formula is to take care of your customer. Pay attention to the small things. Be customer and service-oriented. If you take care of your customer, Ken says, the customer will take care of you. Ken accomplishes this with passion. Incidentally, he also suggests knowing your market. You can't call "everyone" your market. Target the market. Niche it down. Then work your niche. His final comment is one of my favorites. He says *it's far more important to be interested than interesting.* Be interested in everyone you meet. Show interest in their life and family. Ask questions and listen to the answers. Comment on their answer and let them know you are listening. You will be thought of as one in service to your customer.

Ken's philosophy is simple and effective. Anybody could follow it but most people don't. Most people don't want to do that much work to be of service to others. Those who do, experience unimaginable success. It worked for Ken and it will work for you. Give and you will receive. It's simple, but not easy. Remember, no one said service is easy. It's very hard work. Taking care of the small things is often arduous. But the payoff is well worth it.—JB

---

*No thoughtful man ever came to the end of his life, and had time and little space of calm from which to look back upon it, who did not know and acknowledge that it was what he had done unselfishly and for others, and nothing else, that satisfied him in the retrospect, and made him feel that he had played the man.*

—Woodrow Wilson

Service

COACH Lombardi practiced this principle in his own particular way. He sought to make his players the best they could be. His goal was to give his players what they wanted. As a result he received what he wanted—the world championship. If he made his players the best they could be, he would be the best he could be. And he truly was a world champion coach. The formula was simple. He served them by helping them become better players and athletes. They in turn served him by helping him gain the world championship. The same is true in all of life. Render more and better service and you will go further in your career. In fact, you could be a world champion.

By giving to others, you succeed. It creates a win-win relationship. Take this baby step now. Think of how you can give more to your "customer," whomever that may be. Your customer may be your spouse, your children, or your employer. Your customer may be the people you represent or the people you are attempting to sell to. Write down ten things in your success journal you can do to better care for *your* customer. Give more and you will receive more.

Remember, writing things down is only a small step in the process. But it's a vital one. For whatever reason, action is far more likely to be taken if the step is written down first. *Writing* is a baby step. *Taking action* is several steps in the right direction. Remember, people want many things. Some of these may differ according to the individual's needs at the moment. There are several universals however. People generally want to be appreciated. They want to feel included in things. Most would like to be listened to. People usually want sympathetic help on personal problems. And they like recognition. If you want to be of service to others, try any of these.

---

*It is possible to give away and become richer! It is also possible to hold on too tightly and lose everything. Yes, the liberal man shall be rich! By watering others, he waters himself.*
—**Proverbs 11:24-25** LB

# Modeling

MODELING (mod´l-ing) n. 1. A person or object serving as an example to be imitated. 2. Coach Lombardi often spoke of the men who were models in his life. His father was a major one. His college football coach, Jim Crowley, a member of the famed Four Horsemen of Notre Dame was another. The priests who taught him at Fordham were major influences. So was Col. "Red" Blaik at West Point under whom Lombardi worked. NFL legends, George Halas and Paul Brown, were influential later on in his life. Coach Lombardi never stinted in his willingness to give credit to those who provided examples for him to follow.

In my life, I've been very lucky to have the opportunity to work for some outstanding managers, and I'm always saddened when I discover other people who haven't been as fortunate. The people I worked for taught me things I might never have learned on my own. They taught me how to lead, how to follow, how to delegate, and how to deal with difficult people. I learned by watching them, and taking what I liked and thought would work for me. I also learned by observing managers I didn't respect and rejecting their models.

Of course, the greatest role model in my life was my father. He wasn't perfect. He had to be reminded to take out the garbage. He had a temper. He wasn't particularly handy around the house. And he could be inattentive both as a husband and father. But in the bedrock matters—faith, discipline, commitment, work ethic—he was a terrific role model. I can only hope you have been lucky enough to have someone in your life to model after. If you have been so blessed, please understand that in return you have an obligation to model and mentor others when the opportunity arises. It will be a very rewarding experience and hasten you on your road to success.—VL, Jr.

---

*When all is said and done, a leader must exercise an effective influence and the degree he accomplishes this depends upon the personality of the man. The incandescence of which he is capable; the flame which burns within him; the magnetism which draws the hearts of men toward him.*

—Coach Lombardi

## Modeling

ALL successful people have one thing in common. They all have successful role models. Oftentimes they have several role models. These role models can serve many purposes. They show you the trail, give guidance, or simply provide inspiration. The one thing they do best is act as a constant reminder that you can succeed. After all, *they* did.

Coach Lombardi had many models. In return, Coach Lombardi provided an ample model for his football players. Among the few places where role models are automatically built into the system are sports and the military. In these fields, role models are provided automatically. The models are a part of the system and allow the team to continue long past the loss of the coach or the commander. In football successful players and coaches are models. In the military superior officers and NCO's serve the same function.

Modeling is one of the most powerful influences in a person's life. When I wrote books about teenage suicide and drug abuse, I discovered its powers. I discovered the one factor which most effectively predicted suicide attempts in children is depression in the primary caretaker. This is usually the mother. The same influence pervades childhood drug use. The factor which most accurately predicts drug problems in children is tranquilizer or alcohol abuse in the primary caretaker. It's not the peer group, rock music, or even childhood depression. It's what the child sees in the model his parents present. Modeling is magic. Be very selective about who you choose as your model. But choose one. If nothing else, read biographies of people you'd like to emulate. It's even better to have a living, breathing model though. But if that's unrealistic then do the next best thing. It's a baby step on the road to success.—JB

---

*See the way God does things and fall into line. Don't fight the facts of nature.*

—Ecclesiastes 7:13 LB

## Modeling

IN my professional practice I have discovered one unfailing universal truth. Every child abuser I have ever worked with in therapy was abused as a child. I am not saying every person abused as a child will become an abuser. But every *abuser* I have worked with *was abused*.

On television and radio talk shows I am often asked to explain the difference between those that do and don't become abusers. Most people will either become like their model or do the exact opposite. This is true in virtually all extreme situations. Hyper-masculine fathers either raise super-macho sons, or those who totally reject their masculinity. Alcoholics often raise alcohol abusers or teetotalers. They will usually be one extreme or the other. The point is that children often model the extreme behavior—whatever it is—rather than the abusive or addictive behavior.

Modeling is very powerful. The good news is you can change your role model. Take control of your future. Choose your models from this point forward. You didn't choose your parents. They were a biological coincidence. But you can choose your model from this point forward. You will become like your model, so choose very carefully. Remember, the power of modeling is unbelievable. It's the most profound learning you will ever experience. One of the reasons is because most of it is done subconsciously. As a result, your defense mechanisms are lowered. The results are imprinted indelibly into your core. Choose models. But choose them with caution. This is important incidentally, regardless of your age. Modeling doesn't stop at the age of forty, fifty, or sixty. It continues throughout your life. You do have a model. You may not be completely conscious of it. John Wayne died many years ago. But many fifty- or sixty-year-old men still struggle to measure up. Think about it. Take charge. And choose your models carefully.—JB

---

*Children have never been very good at listening to their elders, but they have never failed to imitate them.*

—James Baldwin

## Modeling

ONE of the best places to do positive modeling is with a master-mind group as discussed in the chapter on teamwork. You can develop a mastermind group with people you would like to model. It may not include everyone you would like. But at least you can have some control over who you choose to follow. Modeling is far more powerful than formal learning. Therefore it's extremely important that you choose your mastermind group meticulously. More importantly, be extremely careful with whom you associate. Since modeling is predominantly a subconscious process, you will become like those you associate with.

Begin by taking this baby step. Carefully survey your friendships that work. Take an inventory and list them in your success journal. If you have any friends you don't want to become like, you may need to make a conscious decision to steer away from them. You don't necessarily have to dump these friends, but you can add some new ones. What do you want to do with your life? Choose your models accordingly.

Choose your mastermind group similarly. Attempt to fill it with people you aspire to become like. There are obvious limits. I'd like to have Coach Lombardi in my mastermind group. That can't happen for metaphysical reasons. I'd like to have Vince and several other writers and speakers as well. Geography alone could prevent them from being included. Each of us has to work within the parameters that exist. But you can still choose who you spend your time with. To be a success, model success. The mastermind group is a great place to start. If factors prevent you from doing this physically, model in other ways. Read books like this one. Study biographies of successful people. Watch historical videos. Find someone with the kind of traits you'd like to develop. Then study him or her. Modeling is an important baby step.—JB

---

*Example is the school of mankind, and they will learn at no other.*
—Edmund Burke

# Coach

COACH (koch) n. 1. A person who imparts knowledge and skill to train and prepare students or teams for success. 2. Ask any man who played for Coach Lombardi and he will tell you that Lombardi did the one thing all great coaches do. He created an environment within which the player could succeed. First, he told his players exactly what he expected of them. He painted a picture of what it would look like when they did their job excellently. Then he gave the players everything they needed to succeed, including the tools, the skills, and the training. Finally, Coach Lombardi got out of their way and let them play. Bart Starr said of him, "More than anything else, he wanted us to be great men after we'd left football."

At age forty-seven, when I decided to become a professional speaker, I looked for the names of successful speakers whom I might consult. Time and again one name came up— Mick Delaney. I called Mick and he invited me to his house. Once Mick became convinced I was serious about this career change, he took me under his wing. We spent hours and hours just talking about the speaking profession. The wisdom was his, and I was the sponge. Mick designed my first brochure and he helped me put together my first audio tape. He marketed me to a number of his clients. He introduced me to a number of speakers bureaus, many of whom I still do business with. I will be forever grateful to Mick for the help he gave me during those beginning years. I shudder to think how long it would have taken me to become a successful speaker without his help.

I urge you, in whatever field you're in, to find a mentor and coach. Coaches can be an invaluable asset to you—both personally and in your career. And what return can you make after someone has rendered such valuable assistance to you, as Mick Delaney did for me? Find someone you can coach and mentor.—VL, Jr.

---

*They call it coaching but it is teaching. You do not just tell them . . . you show them the reasons.*
                                                                —**Coach Lombardi**

## Coach

SOME say Michael Jordan is the greatest basketball player to ever play the game. Guess what? He has a coach. So does track athlete Jackie Joyner Kersee. Elizabeth Dole made a resounding speech at the 1996 Republican Convention. She had a coach. So does John Madden when he prepares to go on television. Every champion in every field has a coach. In some cases she might not be called a coach. She might be called a friend, mentor, or teacher. Your coach may be younger, older, or actually less-skilled. After all, Phil Jackson, Michael Jordan's coach, could never defeat him in a game of one-on-one. But he's still there. What's the big deal? Why have a coach? The best reason of all is because it works.

The Dallas Cowboys had the worst season ever the year before they hired Jimmy Johnson. With a change in personnel they were in the playoffs two years later. This turnaround was reminiscent of Coach Lombardi's. Coaching makes a difference. Strong-willed Dallas Cowboy owner, Jerry Jones, decided he still needed a coach for his team after Johnson left. He hired Barry Switzer, who turned the team around and took the them back to the Super Bowl. Obviously, Troy Aikman, Emmitt Smith, and the "Moose" Daryl Johnston are skilled athletes. But they still need a coach. If *they do,* then we all should have one.

Unless you are further along in your chosen field of success than Emmitt Smith or Troy Aikman, go find a coach. You might make more money than your coach. So does Troy. You might be able to beat them in a game of one-on-one. So can Michael. You might be more successful than your coach. So is Libby Dole. But she still needs one. So do you. Coaches play an important role for people who experience success. The relationship does not have to be a formal one, though it can be. It could be a very structured relationship or it might be quite loose. But if you want to succeed, seek a coaching relationship—immediately!

---

*I have taught thee in the way of wisdom; I have led thee in right paths.*

—Proverbs 4:11

Coach

I was one of many young Marines and soldiers in a major battle of the Vietnam War. I was twenty years old and had been in combat on a few occasions. To say I was frightened would be a gross understatement. Two helicopters were shot down, one of which I was riding in a few minutes earlier. F-4 Phantom jets were dropping napalm in the distance. Cobra gunships spread the jungle with gunfire. Rocket propelled grenades and AK-47 gunfire spattered over my head. You never forget the sound of an AK-47. It doesn't go bang, bang, bang! It goes kack, kack, kack!

I found myself seeking shelter behind one of the helicopters which had crashed a few minutes earlier. With me were several soldiers I had never met. One was a Green Beret master sergeant with whom I later became friends. He was a Hungarian refugee whose name even his friends couldn't pronounce. Everybody called him "Herbie." We were pinned down and returning gunfire to an enemy we could not see. I looked up and almost beyond eyesight saw a Huey helicopter circling in a small pattern. I asked Herbie who it was. He looked up and replied, "That's Coach One Zero—the colonel..." He went on to explain that the colonel stayed well above the battle, orbiting to get a better "vision" of events.

As a result of my immaturity, I didn't understand at first. Under my breath I suggested that the colonel come on down and help us out. But later several things became apparent. First of all, his radio call sign—Coach One Zero—was very appropriate. After all, a colonel should be a coach not a rifleman. Additionally, coaches need to have good vision. That's almost impossible when somebody's shooting at you. Fear can prevent you from seeing the big picture. A coach can see the big picture. We needed them in combat and fell woefully short during the Vietnam War. We also need them in life. Get a coach. Capture the vision.—JB

---

*A teacher affects eternity; he can never tell where his influence stops.*

—Henry Adams

## Coach

SOME say a coaching relationship is probably best when it's a formal one, with a written agreement both for reasons of understanding and finance. However, some that are less formal are also effective. In many ways a mentor can be a coach and a model. But you definitely have to pursue them. They don't knock on your door and volunteer their services.

A good coach must be willing to provide objective feedback. He or she needs to know and share your vision. Coach One Zero was a perfect example. He led the battle calmly. He could see ahead and behind. He maintained the big picture while giving good feedback. This could not have been achieved had he been lying wounded on the ground. Coaches seldom play the sport and coach at the same time. There's good reason for that. A good coach keeps the vision, maintains objectivity, and has your best interests at heart. You may have trouble finding such a person. But you need to start.

Take this baby step today. Investigate the possibility of obtaining a professional coach or mentor. If for some reason you can't get professional coaching, then inquire about an informal relationship. Anthony Robbins says, "Success leaves clues." The fact is if someone blazed a trail their path is still there. Look for it. You will find it in biographies, self-help books, and cassettes. Find the path left by successful people around you. Look for their success clues. Make a list in your success journal of the clues a successful person would leave behind. Remember, your coach doesn't have to make more money than you do. She doesn't have to run faster or jump higher. He doesn't have to work in the same occupational field or be of a similar religious persuasion. Don't discriminate due to age, gender, or racial background. Go get a coach.

---

*You cannot teach a man anything; you can only help him to find it within himself.*

—Galileo

# 11

# The Balance
# of
# Success

*There is only one success—to be able to spend your life in your own way.*

—Christopher Morley

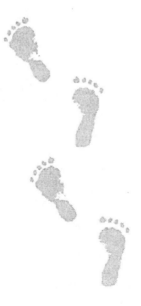

# Control

CONTROL (kon-trol´) 1. To exercise authority or dominating influence over those things you truly can impact. It also involves ignoring those things over which you have no impact. 2. Like many coaches, Lombardi sought to control many of the variables involved in getting a team ready to play a game. He even tried to control the weather. Lombardi installed heating coils underneath the turf at Lambeau field where the Packers played. The idea was that late in the season, when the weather turned cold, the coils would be activated and the field would remain pliant despite the weather. Before the 1967 championship game against the Dallas Cowboys, a game later referred to as the "Ice Bowl," Lombardi anticipated that the coils would keep the field soft. But the day turned so cold—minus thirteen degrees—and windy that the coils failed. By the second half the field was a sheet of ice. Some things even Coach Lombardi couldn't control.

Control is a problem for me. I feel the need to be in control and get frustrated when I can't be. The irony is that we are able to control so little. Try this exercise. Find a straight-back comfortable chair. Put your feet squarely on the floor with your hands folded in your lap. Close your eyes and take three deep breaths letting your breath out slowly. Relax and empty your mind. See how long you can go without a thought about the past, something you need to do today, or an event coming up in the future. Even though it's your intention to control your mind by keeping your mind blank, within moments unwanted thoughts will intrude. This exercise reminds me how little control I can exert over things in my life. I can't even control my thoughts for a few moments!

As a speaker, I often find myself striving to "make a difference" in the lives of my audience. How foolish. I can't exert that kind of control. Only the people in the audience possess the power to change. The only thing I can control is how I deliver my presentation. An affirmation I use when I feel myself in a control mode is, "I'm no longer captain of the world. There's no pay value in being captain of the world. It's either change them or me, and there's too many of them."—VL, Jr.

---

*The good Lord gave you a body that can stand most anything. It's your mind you have to convince.*

—Coach Lombardi

## Control

IN this particular chapter the concept of *control* is not a dirty word or unhealthy concept. Taking control is learning to cope with what you would legitimately have some control over. It doesn't include other people such as your spouse, children, boss, or traffic. It doesn't include things that most people go crazy over. The one thing it does include is yourself.

However, this is what most people ignore. It's much easier to obsess about what you can't control than what you can. The moment you begin to focus on yourself, you have a responsibility to act. Most people don't want to act. It's too much work. You do have control over a few things in your life. This includes things most people have never imagined. You can have a degree of control over your blood pressure, your heart rate, and the way you react to pain. You can even control the way you react to your emotions. Believe it or not, you can actually control your weight. At times, you might swear that's impossible. But it's not only possible. It's the truth.

You can take "control of your life"—not someone else's life. Certainly you can't control Mother Nature, the Cosmic Consciousness, or the universe. But you can control *your* life. Focus on yourself. Learn to control your impulses, your anger, and your success. You can't control the weather, but you can control your reaction to it. You can't control your spouse. But you can control how you treat him or her. You can't control the IRS. You can control whether or not you file your taxes on time. You can't control your children. But you can control whether or not you say how much you love them. You can take control of *your* life, but only yours. Don't do the common thing. Don't make the common mistake. Forget about focusing on other people, or even other things. Control *yourself*. That's enough for a lifetime. It's a major baby step on the road to success.

---

*He is most powerful who has power over himself.*

—Seneca

## Control

MOST people find big emotional catastrophes more easily controlled in the long run than everyday stress. If your house burns down, there's a death in the family, or someone has cancer—resources become mobilized to help you. People reach out to you. Professionals will intervene. Though these difficulties are potentially overwhelming, other people help you. Their presence makes it easier.

The biggest problem is not losing control during the major crises. It's the everyday conflicts—traffic problems, telephone interruptions, and problems with children—that cause problems. These are the kinds of things that catch you unprepared with your defense mechanisms lowered. Somebody cuts you off on the freeway and you try to chase them down. The telephone rings when you least need it to and you jerk it out of the wall. You go on a family vacation and get so stressed, you can't wait to get home. These are often the times when you "lose it."

I have one friend who works in an extremely stressful job. Occasionally when he comes home, he needs to be left alone. He bought a baseball cap with an old flag on it that warns, "*Don't Tread On Me.*" He decided to use the cap as a warning signal to other family members. When the family sees him wearing the cap they cut him a wide berth. After he decompresses for a few minutes, he takes it off and rejoins the clan. He's taken responsibility for his emotions. We all need to do the same. You can control your life. You can begin by taking responsibility for yourself. If you're having a bad day, do something about it. If somebody else is having a bad day, don't let it ruin yours. You can control your life. However you can't do anything about someone else's.—JB

---

*And he that ruleth his spirit (is better) than he that taketh a city.*
—**Proverbs 16:32b**

## Control

YOU'LL be relaxed and successful to the degree you have a sense of control over what is happening in your life. You begin to experience control the moment you take action. Changing your life means pursuing new goals. At other times it means walking away from a "lose-lose situation." It also means focusing on yourself.

Speaker and consultant Jim Cathcart commented on this subject recently. When considering an action step, he suggested asking yourself the following questions. *What would the person I want to become do in this situation? How would the person I want to become act? What would he or she say and do?* Think about it. Then do it. You will take control of your life.

All the skills we've discussed up to this point are necessary to successfully take control. Goals, planning, and good coaching are vital. Without action, however, it amounts to just fantasy. To take control you must do something. Therefore, take this baby step today. Review the goals you have established to this point. In your success journal, list daily action steps for each goal. Don't let a day go by that you don't take some step—even if it's a small one—toward completing a major goal. It can be a phone call, a letter, a discussion or even a learning experience. But do *something.* You can take control of yourself. You can take control of your life. Do it by taking one baby step at a time.

---

*The secret of all success is to know how to deny yourself. Prove that you can control yourself, and you are an educated man; and without this all other education is good for nothing.*
                                                              —R.D. Hitchcock

# Leadership

LEADERSHIP (le´-der-ship) n. 1. The capacity to be a leader; ability to lead. 2. When Coach Lombardi joined the New York Giants as an assistant coach in 1954, he brought a reputation of having been an outstanding high school and college coach, but he was new to pro football. He might have taken the attitude, "I'm the coach, you do it *my* way." Instead, he chose to listen to the players—the mark of every great leader. During his first training camp, after the evening meeting, Lombardi would wander up to the players' dorm and talk strategy. They would discuss how a play could be run better. Once they grasped that Lombardi was sincere in seeking their advice, the veterans responded and shared their experience. Despite his reputation, Coach Lombardi was a leader who communicated with his people.

Not long ago I wrote a book called, *Coaching for Teamwork: Winning Concepts for Business in the Twenty-First Century*. In the book I described the qualities most leaders possess. They are: (1) An inspiring vision and the communication skills to transmit the vision to their people. (2) The communication skills to build a consensus—to get people to work together to achieve the vision. (3) The communication skills to engender enthusiasm within their team to achieve the vision. (4) A willingness to lead.

Understand, we're not talking about the ability to communicate. We all have that—but the willingness to communicate. It's the *willingness* of a leader to "haul" herself out of her office and talk and listen to her people that makes a difference. Today's work force is demanding that leaders communicate. People are flooded with information today from sources such as *CNN, C-Span, America On Line*, talk radio, *USA Today*, other newspapers and magazines, and computer networks. They have come to expect the same information flow at work. When workers don't get timely, up-to-date information in their workplace, they fill the vacuum with the one thing a leader doesn't want—rumor based on misinformation.—VL, Jr.

---

*Leadership is based on a spiritual quality; the power to inspire, the power to inspire others to follow.*
—Coach Lombardi

## Leadership

PARTICIPANTS in leadership programs are often asked to rate leaders they worked for, from worst to best. The "worst" list usually includes leaders described as flamboyant or "screamers." Interestingly, most groups never identify one of these on their list of "best" leaders.

Those that constantly surface and rise to the top are from a different cut. There are no gurus or cult leaders on this list. The best are usually the hardest workers in the group. Coach Lombardi stated that leaders are made by hard effort and hard work. He went on to clarify that "This new leadership is in sacrifice, self denial . . . and love . . . it is in fearlessness, humility, and the perfectly disciplined will." Such characteristics are rarely found among the many "wannabees" who aspire to be the modern gurus of leadership.

Leadership is not necessarily pretty! It's work! Lombardi's "new leadership" is not in giving orders. It's in "living." Our society is thirsting for this new leadership on all fronts. From marriages and families to corporations and government, our society is void of real leadership. This emptiness is profound and shocking. And to make it even worse, children are growing up with painfully few leadership role models. ". . . Sacrifice, self denial, love, humility, the perfectly disciplined will . . ." is quite an order. It's also a requirement if you're going to lead for success. Start living this model today. New leaders are needed. Don't hesitate to apply for the job. The requirements are within this chapter. If you're interested, sign up.

---

*A platoon leader doesn't get his platoon to go by getting up and shouting, 'I am smarter, I am bigger, I am stronger, I am the leader.' He gets men to go along with him because they want to do it for him and they believe in him.*

—Dwight D. Eisenhower

## Leadership

IN the 1996 college football season, Tennessee's game of the year did not occur in the post-season bowlfest. In fact, the peak came unfortunately early in the season. Pre-season polls had touted UT quarterback Peyton Manning as a shoo-in for the Heisman trophy. The (University of Tennessee) football team was predicted as a major contender for the national championship.

College football is an obsession in the Southeast. But I've never been anywhere when a state was quite as inspired as the day Tennessee faced Florida. Fans not only had revenge on their minds but a national championship within their grasp. The fever had percolated at a low grade for three years. But it ended in the course of ten brief minutes. By the end of the first quarter the Gators were up 21 to 0. Some of the record-setting 170,000 fans were already leaving. The final score was anti-climactic. UT's fans had an outbreak of big orange depression and talk shows were already discussing "next year."

Most people wonder what went wrong. Backyard quarterbacks, including this one, had a lot of theories. Mine were simple. UT's head coach, Phil Fulmer, is a tremendous recruiter, technician, and head football coach. Steve Spurrier, the Gator head coach, is an ingenious strategist, chess player, and leader. Guess what? The leader won. There's no doubt in my mind that Phil Fulmer would win in arm-wrestling, tackling drills, bench press, or even a personality contest. He's extremely likable, has great rapport with his players, and is incredible at public relations. All of those are fine qualities. In fact, I'd rather have Fulmer as a friend. I trust him more. But the strategist, chess player, and leader won. He led for success. You can too. There's an interesting footnote to this story. In March 1997 Peyton Manning announced he would return to the University of Tennessee for his fourth season. The armchair quarterbacks were already talking about "skinning the swamp lizard!" Spurrier, on the other hand, looks at the chess board and contemplates the next move.—JB

---

*Reason and judgment are the qualities of a leader.*

—Tacitus

Leadership

THE realities of leadership are several. Truth number one is: No one style works all the time with everybody. Truth number two is: What works with a person on one occasion will not necessarily work at another time, even though it's the same person. Truth number three is: Even though a style is successful with one group on one occasion does not mean the same style will work with another group under the same circumstances.

The equation of leadership is partially defined by the leader. But it's the leader's ability to adapt to the situation that is the most important quality. Coach Lombardi's relationship with Jerry Kramer has been discussed in various books. During a practice session Lombardi called Kramer "a cow" and said he was the worst football player he had ever seen. Later Kramer sat in the locker room dejected. Some said he was crying. Coach Lombardi approached him and told Kramer that some day he was going to be one of the greatest guards in the league. He'd gotten Kramer's attention by the first approach. He inspired him by the second.

Coach Lombardi said a leader is composed of a blend of many qualities adapted to the individual personality and manifested by hard work. Take this baby step today. In your success journal define your own leadership style. How can you adapt it personally and situationally to help you become a leader in all circumstances? Study it. Refine it. Define your own philosophy of leadership. By doing so, you will experience success. You may say you don't have leadership style. Begin to develop one. You're closer than you think. It's a baby step on the road to success.

---

*Give therefore thy servant an understanding heart to judge thy people, that I may discern between good and bad.*

—1 Kings 3:9

# Laughter

LAUGHTER (laf ´ter) n. 1. The expression of mirth by a series of inarticulate sounds, characteristically with the mouth open in a wide smile. 2. Coach Lombardi's laugh wasn't so much a belly laugh as an all over body laugh. Lombardi laughed hardest at his own jokes, which often weren't that funny. But his laugh was so infectious that you found yourself laughing right along with him. Lombardi's emotions were never far below the surface. He could laugh and cry in the same conversation.

"Laugh, and the world laughs with you; weep, and you weep alone," a quote attributed to Ella Wheeler Wilcox, rings true doesn't it? Speakers are constantly told, if you want to be paid, make them laugh. Your message may be serious, but if you want your audience to remember you and your message, use humor.

Don't you love being around people who make you laugh? We gravitate toward people who make us laugh. I know I do. My wife and I just spent a few days with my closest friend and his wife. I was best man at his wedding and he was best man at mine. Why are we such good friends? Lots of reasons, but a major one is we laugh. Laughter is healthy. Studies show that laughter is good medicine. Laughter lowers blood pressure, bolsters the immune system, and alleviates stress. The average child laughs hundreds of times a day. Adults, on average, laugh a dozen times a day. Find some of those lost laughs from childhood and use them for health and success.—VL, Jr.

---

*. . . he'd (Coach Lombardi) go out there and get his troops around him. He laughed. He cried. He prayed. He motivated. I think he could motivate almost anybody to do almost anything. He communicated with human emotions.*

**—Chuck Lane,** Green Bay Packer Publicity Director

Laughter

AS a child I spent most of my time with my grandparents. They were both wonderful and loving people. My grandfather didn't have much of an education, but he was kind, generous, and possessed a great sense of humor. He would often tell me in his own unique way, ". . . laugh hard, Johnny, laugh hard . . ." In spite of difficulties faced, I've followed his advice. It has helped me through a lot of rough times.

My grandpa's sense of humor bordered on vaudevillian. He would probably be considered slapstick or corny by today's standards. He would ask me, "Why did the chicken cross the road?" and had infinite reasons why—none of which I ever got right. He had hundreds of knock-knock jokes and practiced his reading skills by reading the funny papers to me. He is the first person ever to say, "Pull my finger, Johnny." The resulting expulsion and laughter always resulted in my grandmother and mother chastising both of us. I loved my grandfather and have written about him in all of my books. To say I adored him would be understatement. Grandpa gave me many different gifts. Few of them involved money or material things. Instead, my grandfather gave me love, relationships, a model for life, and a model for death. But the greatest of all these was the advice and gift to "laugh hard." It has been a great stress reliever, a big part of any success I have experienced, and has become my friend. Laugh hard. It will help you on the journey to success.

Go out of your way to laugh if you have to. Read humorous books by the late Lewis Grizzard or Dave Barry. Listen to radio programs that make you pull off the side of the road and guffaw. Syndicated programs such as *Gary Burbank*, *John Boy and Billy*, and *Rick and Bubba*, have all had that effect on me. Obtain audios and videos that create laughter for you. Go to comedy clubs. Do what it takes to laugh hard daily.—JB

---

*A merry heart maketh a cheerful countenance.*
                                                    **—Proverbs 15:13a**

## Laughter

SEVERAL years ago Bob, a friend of mine, was diagnosed with Hodgkin's disease. Hodgkin's is a form of cancer. It can be fatal. It can also be curable. I was first told by a mutual friend about Bob's diagnosis. I made a lunch appointment with him and began contemplating what I would say. Through my experience working with cancer patients, I have learned the first few weeks after the diagnosis are the most important.

I have worked as a psychotherapist with terminal patients for years. I have learned from these cases how important attitude is. Whether it's with cancer patients, victims of heart attacks, or other terminal illness, attitudes often affect the prognosis. It was Norman Cousins who I first heard speak about this. He declared it was best to accept, in terminal cases, the physician's diagnosis but not necessarily the prognosis. Science has demonstrated that emotional attitude, especially a good sense of humor, can often determine whether you'll live or die.

I took this awareness to my lunch appointment with Bob. We greeted each other warmly. He broke the ice by asking if I'd heard about his Hodgkin's. I nodded my head and told him I would be happy to help him recover from it. But first he would have to convince me he was going to live. I explained that this decision was without doubt the most important one he would ever make. He was surprised and assured me we were on the same wave length. He told me he intended to live and had much to live for. I recommended a lengthy program to improve his attitude. I told him of the work of Dr. Bernie Siegel, Norman Cousins, and others on how attitude and humor affect healing. My friend began a concentrated program. He laughed hard. And he survived.—JB

---

*Laughter is a form of internal jogging. It moves your internal organs around. It enhances respiration. It is an igniter of great expectations.*
—Norman Cousins

Laughter

HUMOR has played a significant role in all cultures throughout history in ways that at times were almost holy. In some cultures, to make others laugh is seen as a religious function and considered to be a gift from God. Court jesters were counselors to kings. Roman conquerors had the equivalent of comedians who accompanied them and made fun of the conquering general as part of their task. It was the Roman way of preventing a general's success from going to his head. Laughing helped people keep perspective.

What makes people laugh in one setting may not necessarily work in another. But the benefits of humor penetrate all boundaries and recognize no barriers. Laughter improves lung capacity, brain function, cardiovascular endurance, stomach and intestine function, liver function, kidney function, learning and memory retention, and immune system efficiency. It also provides an anti-depressant effect and regulates mood swings. The benefits of laughter are now compared to that of a miracle drug. I call it "God's anti-depressant." It's inexpensive, easy to swallow, and there are no known adverse side effects. So laugh hard.

Take this baby step today. Put laughter in your life. Yes, get medical treatment. Yes, get exercise. Yes, take care of yourself. But also, make a goal of laughing hard at least three times per day. Visit comedy clubs. They aren't bars. They're psychiatric hospitals for the functional and dysfunctional in all of us. Laugh hard. It'll lengthen your life expectancy and give you success in the short and long term.

---

*The most wasted day of all is that on which we have not laughed.*
—Nicholas Chamfort

# Balance

BALANCE (bal´ens) n. 1. A harmonious arrangement of equilibrium or stability. 2. Coach Lombardi's life and career provide many excellent examples of the qualities successful people possess, but balance was a tough one for him. He did not stint in his commitment to the task at hand. And as both coach and general manager of the Green Bay Packers, he had many tasks before him. Football consumed him for seven months of the year. His duties as general manager occupied him for the other five months. Perhaps that's one reason why he died at age fifty-seven.

Everybody talks about balance. But how many of us are making an honest attempt to do something about it? We're not human "doings," we're human beings. Yet it's so tempting to be constantly "doing" something. This is certainly one pathway to success. But what is your definition of success? I've known football coaches who, if the subject strayed from football, couldn't carry on a conversation. You've got to admire their dedication, but they were boring! You undoubtedly know these kinds of people. Perhaps you recognize a little of this in yourself.

Balance may be more difficult to achieve than any other quality in this book. We have so many demands on us as wage earners, parents, spouses. Where will we find the time for the activities that provide balance? Something that takes up time in your life now, will probably have to go. Personally, I make sure there is time in my life to pray, exercise, read, and spend time with my wife and family. Some weeks I'm more successful than others. Balance is tricky. We feel guilty when we're working. (I should be spending time with my family.) We feel guilty when we're doing something to provide balance. (I should be working.) Where's the balance in balance?—VL, Jr.

---

*It takes a special kind of character to know when to let up, when to back off. He (Coach Lombardi) would get them to the point when they were just about ready to do anything and then he was able to crack a joke or he was able to do something to break the tension and put them back on the right track.*

*—Tom Landry*

Balance

A Hindu proverb says, "Even nectar is poison if taken to excess." One of the greatest challenges to anyone's success is remaining balanced and diversified. Some people illustrate the need for this principle to the point of nausea. Whatever they do is to excess. "Nothing in moderation" is their mantra. To them, if anything is worth doing, it's worth overdoing. It matters little whether it's working, exercising, or drinking. Their motto is "all things to excess."

This path always leads to burnout, pain, and self-sabotage. And it does so, usually quite prematurely. Like a comet, these people burn brightly for a season and just as quickly are gone. Their intense focus becomes an unhealthy obsession. Other aspects of their lives are blocked out. Balance is lost and there is no diversity. They focus intensely on what the goal of the moment is. It briefly becomes the most important thing in their lives. Then they soon tire of it and go on to something else.

There is a better way. Diversify and build your life. By diversifying you don't dilute focus. It doesn't weaken your goals and efforts. It strengthens them by helping you avoid tunnel vision and missing the obvious. It does no good to achieve your goals of financial success and lose your family. It's counterproductive to be successful in your career and die from a heart attack. Diversifying will help you balance your energy and effort, and increase your life expectancy. It will also help you increase your *success expectancy.*

--------

*You should not have a favorite weapon. To become over-familiar with one weapon is as much a fault as not knowing it sufficiently well. You should not copy others, but use weapons which you can handle properly . . . These are things you must learn thoroughly.*
                                                    —Miyamoto Musashi

## Balance

I'M often contacted by radio and television stations to discuss why otherwise high-achieving and successful people make self-destructive decisions. Occasionally these performers are arrested. Other times they are fired, overdose, or commit suicide. I am usually contacted because of several books I've written investigating this problem. Usually by the time the interview is over I will be discussing the importance of balance.

The fact is high achievers are clearly somewhat obsessive-compulsive anyway. To experience high levels of success requires an intense, focused energy that borders on obsessiveness. By the nature of their energy level these people are usually on a tightrope. It's a double-edged sword. To achieve massive success they must focus somewhat obsessively. Yet it's only a small degree of higher focus that will destroy them. Those who walk the tightrope successfully are the ones who not only balance their lives but diversify.

This is the difference between Evander Holyfield and Mike Tyson. Evander has been a Sunday School teacher, motivational speaker, preacher, father, and boxer. Mike Tyson is a boxer. Jimmy Carter has been a farmer, naval officer, construction worker, governor, writer, Sunday School teacher, and politician. Richard Nixon was a politician. Tom Landry was the only football coach the Dallas Cowboys ever had before he retired. Bear Bryant defined college coaching in Alabama up to his retirement. Tom went on to other endeavors. Bear Bryant retired and died. Diversification is vital not only to your health but to your performance. All high performers throughout history, including Thomas Jefferson, Michelangelo, Goethe, Phidias, Da Vinci, and many others, were extremely diverse individuals. It can work for your success as well.—JB

---

*Beware of the man of one book.*
—St. Thomas Aquinas

Balance

IT could be that somebody said it before. But Coach Lombardi is the first person we know of who is quoted as saying, "Fatigue makes cowards of us all." He believed physical conditioning was essential to any occupation. He was correct. Today the preventive health and wellness movement is a major influence in hospitals, insurance companies, and among politicians. In fact, some suggest it will be the next major medical specialty.

Physical health is an important part of balance and diversity. And it's far more than getting your illness treated. In fact, health is an active process of doing what's necessary to avoid illness whenever possible. When it's not possible to avoid illness, healthy people recover quickly after treatment. This involves exercising your body and your mind. It includes resting adequately, eating properly, and working on something of meaning to you. It involves all of the things we've discussed.

Take this baby step today. Work on scheduling your life to achieve the balance you need. In your success journal, schedule daily periods of each factor already mentioned. Try your schedule for several weeks. Then you can make the decision about how to adjust it for the future. Continue to make adjustments until you have a sense of diversity and balance in your life. At this point you will begin experiencing the foundations for long-term and lasting success. My grandfather used to say that balance is a "holy word." I'm sure it is. It's difficult to balance the drive necessary to achieve great things with the necessity to back off and take a break on a regular basis. But such balance is your goal. Practicing balance will help you prolong your success.

---

*I have become all things to all men so that by all possible means I might save some.*

*—1 Corinthians 9:22 NIV*

# 12

# The Breath of God

*Success abides longer among men when it is planned by the hand of God.*

—Pindar

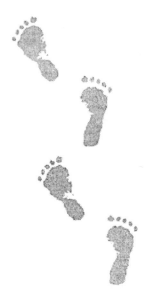

# Duck

DUCK (duk) v. 1. To lower your head quickly to avoid injury from oncoming projectiles. To avoid a potentially painful situation or remove yourself by getting out of harm's way. Many people fail to duck until they've had enough pain. 2. Sometimes Coach Lombardi ducked. Sometimes he didn't and later wished he had. Immediately after a game when his emotions were close to the surface, he would angrily respond to a question he considered less than intelligent. The only thing he accomplished was to earn the enmity of that particular reporter. The writers who covered the Packers on a regular basis came to understand that Lombardi meant nothing personal by his outbursts. He barked at everyone. But if Coach Lombardi had ducked a little more often, he could have saved himself a lot of anguish.

Bud Grant, the very successful coach of the Minnesota Vikings, liked sparring with reporters no more than Lombardi, but was more stoic in his replies. He once suggested this response to press criticism: Rather than reply, he said, stuff a rag in your mouth and lie down behind a big log until things blow over. This is sound advice, not only for those in the public eye, but for all of us. We are all going to take some shots over the course of our lives, some of them justified, some of them not.

As with so many things, we have a choice. We can respond out of anger, and say something we will later regret, remembering that words once uttered can never be taken back. Or we can stuff a rag in our mouth and go lie down behind a big log until our wounds heal—at least until we're able to take a calm, reasoned approach to the criticism.—VL, Jr.

---

*He (Coach Lombardi) had a hard exterior but he also had a big, soft heart.*

—**Ray Nitschke,** Linebacker, Green Bay Packers

## Duck

THE reality is the more successful you become, the more envy and animosity you'll generate. Author Neil Simon said, "Success breeds jealousy, and jealousy breeds contempt." A few people in particular and society in general will develop a love/hate relationship with you as you experience even further success. This is true, whether you're a football player, business person, or a stay-at-home mom.

Coach Lombardi, like many others before him who experienced success, had more than his share of detractors. Even though they may not have intended to hurt him personally, detractors can take their toll. Social scientists say well over ninety-eight percent of things that happen to you are not personally intended. The people who "take shots" may not even know you. Perhaps they just know about you. Believe the scientists. Remember that ninety-eight percent of things that hurt you aren't directed at you as an individual. At the same time, it's important that you remember to duck.

Many people make the mistake of wondering why someone might be attempting to hurt them. Actually going through this process can make the pain even worse. Don't ask why! Just duck! Remove yourself from any situation that results in great pain. And then forget it. What these people do will never be logical. Don't make the mistake of trying to make sense out of that which is nonsense or vice versa. Let go of it. Get away from it. If you sit around and analyze the "why" of it, you will possibly be hurt even more. Understanding is often a luxury you can't afford. So don't take it personally. But at the same time, don't be a target. Remove yourself quietly from the line of fire. Don't forget to duck.

---

*There are no statues built to memorialize critics. They don't get monuments.*

—Bill Gove

### Duck

I was wounded twice during the Vietnam War. The first time was painful but otherwise insignificant. The second time, however, was far more memorable. The man who shot me was standing six feet away. We were making eye contact. He was pointing a 9 mm. pistol at me. He was wearing a light green helmet with a red star in the middle. I'll never forget his face.

He pulled the trigger. The bullet went through my left shoulder and knocked me several steps backward. I fell to the ground. Then, the man who shot me walked up and said something I didn't understand in Vietnamese. Then I passed out. They say that when you're about to die your life passes before your eyes. This was what happened to me. I thought I was dying. When I finally did wake up days later, I was in the hospital.

For years I had nightmares about that experience. The face of the man who shot me haunted my dreams and my days. For the first time in my life I truly hated another person. I wanted to hurt him. At times I wanted to kill him. I agonized over my physical pain. However the real agony was my emotional wounds. Eventually I sought psychotherapy. Then I began to realize his attack wasn't personal at all. The moment I began to understand that, was the moment I began to heal. He couldn't have meant it personally. He didn't even know me. He was shooting at my uniform and if I could have, I would have shot at his. But I didn't know him either. I wasn't angry at him and he wasn't angry at me. We didn't even know each other. I made a mistake. I forgot to duck. It wasn't personal but it still hurt. If you can avoid it don't make that mistake. Don't forget to duck. If you can't, don't take it personally. It won't make the physical pain go away. But it will help you avoid a lot of unnecessary emotional pain.—JB

---

*Rest satisfied with doing well, and leave others to talk of you as they please.*

—**Pythagoras**

<u>Duck</u>

MANY people have learned this baby step the hard way. Nothing will teach you to duck better than intense pain. But you don't have to get shot to learn its significance. Pain is a great teacher. However we'd rather get along without it.

Instead, we encourage you to develop a low pain threshold. Learn from other people's mistakes. Reverend Winford Hendrix, a good friend, used to say he would rather learn from other people's mistakes. He didn't have time to make them all himself. That's a great philosophy. When you learn to duck, you can avoid some of the pain that other people experience. We highly recommend it.

Take this baby step today. Think of times when you've taken things personally that weren't intended that way. There may be many occasions, or only a few, but list them in your success journal. Then make a second list. Recall occasions you didn't duck but should have. Remember, very little is intended personally. However the "shots" still cause pain. Most people make the mistake of not ducking and then feeling sorry for themselves because it hurts. Remember—forgetting to duck means you consciously or unconsciously didn't avoid a painful situation when you could have. There's a better idea. Don't forget to duck. Forgive yourself and everyone else for whatever's happened in the past. It's over. Release it. Then think only of today and the future. When people hurt you intentionally or unintentionally—duck. Don't ask why. Don't try to understand. Don't worry about figuring it out. Just duck and get out of the way. Then go on with your life. It's a baby step to success.

---

*Do not let any unwholesome talk come out of your mouths, but only what is helpful for building others up according to their needs, that it may benefit those who listen.*

                                        —Ephesians 4:29 NIV

# Changing Course

CHANGING COURSE (chanj´ing kors) v. n. 1. To alter the direction of continuing movement. 2. Coach Lombardi knew how to change course. Lombardi and his coaching staff would labor over a game plan for long hours each week, studying film and the tendencies of the next opponent. But each game would bring changes from the predictable. The opposition, after all, had done some of their own planning, and adjustments would need to be made. These course changes would be made at half time when everyone had a chance to calm down. Then the staff, with input from the players, would make adjustments that most often led to victory in the second half.

Have you ever tried to balance on a bicycle without peddling? You will fall over. To avoid falling you need to start peddling to be in motion. Once under way and in motion, it's easy to change course. However, this wasn't the case when you were young and learning to ride your bike. You'd be going down the road, a little shaky and up ahead you'd see a rock. You'd concentrate on the rock because you didn't want to hit it. You kept on focusing on the rock—so what happened? You hit the rock!

Life is like riding a bike. If you're not in motion you fall. But if you're in motion pursuing a goal, it's easy to change course unless you're looking at the rock. If your focus is so narrow that you can't see anything else around you, you will fall just as surely as if you were trying to balance on a stationary bicycle. So set yourself in motion pursuing a goal. Scan your surroundings constantly. Look for possible danger. But also keep your eyes open for opportunities that might call for a change in course.—VL, Jr.

---

*The spirit, the will to win, and the will to excel—these are the things that endure and these are the qualities that are so much more important than any of the events that occasion them.*

—Coach Lombardi

Changing Course

MANY years ago I was in a business relationship that was very happy and rewarding to me. I literally loved my partners. I considered them more family than associates. During this relationship I began writing my first two books. As a result I found myself traveling, speaking, and appearing on radio and television. Although I didn't know it at the time, this ultimately led to some problems. My partners had difficulty with my new schedule. They began complaining that I wasn't available enough and asked me to leave the partnership. We had several discussions as a group, and I continued to ask how we could compromise and keep the partnership together. Ultimately I was forced to leave.

This was very painful to me, and I discussed it with a friend who eventually asked me a very important question. He asked why I would want to be a part of an organization that obviously didn't want me as a member. "If the horse is dead, John. Quit riding it. It isn't going anywhere." That wasn't the first time I had heard that phrase. But it was the first time it had ever been applied to me. It helped me realize the truth of my situation. It was painful to dismount. But it was also very healthy. It opened up incredible opportunities for my life, which I would otherwise never have noticed.

The same adage is true for you. If the horse is dead, dismount. Sometimes you have to change course. It may not be obvious to you. My love for my partners blinded me to what was actually occurring. An objective friend enlightened me. But my friend was truly objective. He had nothing to gain from my decision. Seek objective feedback before you change course. But do ensure the feedback is truly objective.—JB

---

*Always listen to experts. They'll tell you what can't be done and why. Then do it.*

—Robert Heinlein

## Changing Course

THIS is not the opposite of the chapter on motivation. True motivation is invaluable and important. But being motivated about the right thing is essential. It's important to look at the object of your motivation. If you are highly motivated to overdrink, as an example, you're not necessarily moving toward the right goal.

Several years ago the *Atlanta Constitution* reported a story about a lady who attended some highly-motivating religious meetings. Apparently the revival turned out to be an "irreligious" cult; but nevertheless she was highly motivated at the conclusion of the meeting. She had been inspired to be more submissive to her husband. Two days later she watched as her husband beat their son to death. She explained to the reporter that she was justified in letting her husband do this because she was "submitting to her husband and God's will." She was highly-motivated. In fact, she was intoxicated with motivation. But she was after the wrong goal. Tragically, her son is dead.

Take a good look at your own life. You could be highly-motivated but pursuing the wrong dream. Or perhaps you are pursuing the right thing but the "horse is dead." If it is, dismount. Getting off the horse may be sad, unfortunate, or even painful. But if it is dead you need to find another motivation. I believe in motivation but I don't believe in insanity. Sometimes you need to change course. If the course you are on doesn't lead to a worthwhile goal perhaps you need to change.

---

*Your chances of success are directly proportional to the degree of pleasure you derive from what you do. If you are in a job you hate, face the fact squarely and get out.*

—*Michael Korda*

## Changing Course

COACH Lombardi practiced this principle, though he may never have articulated it in these words. On several occasions he rode the horse as far as it would take him, then dismounted and rode another. As a high school coach at St. Cecilia High School, he took the basketball team to a state championship. He had never played the sport, but he coached it. He also coached the baseball and football teams. Then he moved on.

At one point in his life he was a seminary student and had plans to be a priest. But he decided this was not the opportunity he wanted to pursue. He found another horse to ride. He was a college coach and assistant coach at the professional level. He rode those horses as far as they could carry him. But he didn't ride them into the ground and neither should you.

People often enjoy the metaphor of this baby step, but they get confused about its practical application. This is understandable. The concept is a very personal and emotional one. The equation is this. If you're involved in any activity, habit, or relationship that is self-destructive, you need to make a thorough examination of it. Take this baby step today. Examine your life closely. Look at it comprehensively. In your journal, make a list of any horse you may be riding beyond the time of its death. Evaluate all your involvements very closely, though it may be extremely difficult. It may be important for you to dismount from some of the horses you have been riding. It may not be easy if you choose to do so. But it will expedite your success. Take this baby step slowly and cautiously. Seek the objective, intelligent feedback of someone you trust, who has nothing to gain if you decide to "dismount." There are things you need to give up. But be certain which ones they are. It's a baby step to success.

———————

*Do not lie to each other, since you have taken off your old self with its practices and have put on the new self, which is being renewed in knowledge in the image of its Creater.*

—Colossians 3:9-10 NIV

# Faith

FAITH (fath) n. 1. A confident belief in the truth, value, or trustworthiness of a person, idea, or thing. 2. Coach Lombardi was a deeply religious man. He went to mass and communion on a daily basis. During difficult times Lombardi drew strength from his faith in God. He didn't wear his faith on his sleeve, but he didn't hide it, either. Lombardi was an assistant coach at the U.S. Military Academy for five years (1949-1954). An officer at the Academy, after seeing Lombardi depart for mass every morning and observing him in other situations, went to a priest and asked for instruction in the Catholic faith with the words, "I want to be a Catholic like Vince Lombardi."

"You gotta believe!" has been a rallying cry for many sports teams, beginning with the 1969 World Series Champion New York Mets. It can be your rallying cry. Belief or faith can take many forms. Belief in yourself is the basis for everything you achieve in life. You cannot, on a consistent basis, outperform your belief system. Your self-belief or faith, defines in a very firm way the parameters of your success. This is also true on a societal level. Faith is the collective moral and ethical basis for our progress as a nation. Without the trust and respect that flows from this belief, our social institutions could not function.

Then there is spiritual faith. You might call it God, the infinite, the unknowable, or a higher power. You may choose to ignore this aspect of your humanity. But what you can't do is deny it. You are spiritual by nature and many of life's problems, stress, and illness arise from a denial of the spiritual side of humanity. In truth, there is no situation that is not in some manner spiritual. Every decision you make, every feeling you have, every relationship you nurture has a spiritual dimension. The very essence of life—the growth in wisdom and love—is spiritual. Sooner or later, most people come to this realization. Usually in our late 40's or 50's, after seeking joy and fulfillment in everything else—possessions, power, control, prestige—and finding them wanting, we are ready to admit that true joy lies in faith and the spiritual journey.—VL, Jr.

---

*I firmly believe that any man's finest hour is that moment when he has worked his heart out in a good cause and lies exhausted on the field of battle, victorious.*

—Coach Lombardi

Faith
-

FAITH in yourself originates from constant and repetitive mental and physical practice. This can consume hours, weeks, and even years of work and dedication to something you consider worthwhile. It may begin only as an imagined or visualized goal that seems out of reach. There is nothing wrong with beginning at that point. Yet experience and smaller successes will follow even if you begin with visualization alone with no experience to build from.

In time the confidence you have in yourself will begin to lead to *faith* in your ability to achieve any worthwhile endeavor. The internal confidence becomes the externalized *faith* in other things. The more you practice the stronger it becomes and the more you achieve. This has a self-perpetuating effect that influences your confidence even more.

Over time you begin to expect to win. You begin to assume great results will occur in your life. It can become a self-fulfilling prophecy. You believe in yourself and have faith in the results so strongly that sheer confidence creates the outcome. This is the power of conviction and it can begin in your life today. Faith is not naive, blind, or for the gullible. Anyone can be a cynic. It's easy to develop doubt and skepticism. Faith requires courage, practice, and discipline. It is the sign of a mature mind. Practice your faith. Build it. Condition it. You will soon find yourself experiencing far more success than you ever imagined. With this success other things will also become clear. One of them is that faith can exceed the boundaries of your intellect. The "leap of faith" is exactly what it describes. It goes beyond intellect. Take the leap. Believe in yourself. Believe and conceive. Then achieve, and you can see what you had earlier believed.

---

*Faith is to believe what we do not see; and the reward of faith is to see what we believe.*

—St. Augustine

## Faith

CONFIDENCE in yourself will lead to faith in the outcome of your endeavors. Such faith is contagious. It can influence not only yourself but other people as well. Positive results can occur in other peoples' lives as a result of your own individual faith. Your confidence and faith in another can literally "infect" them so they begin to believe in themselves.

A good friend of mine, who had been out of the work force for over a dozen years unexpectedly was forced to reenter the workplace. Though well-educated and highly-skilled, her self-confidence was extremely low. She took the first opportunity for employment she could find and was not only underappreciated but grossly underpaid. On several occasions her fiancé and I discussed this and finally decided to have a pep talk with her. We began by complimenting her willingness to reenter the work force. We expressed a great deal of respect and admiration for what she was attempting to do. We assured her that we weren't being critical, yet at the same time strongly encouraged her to take on more challenges. With her great personality, she could have been an asset to any sales organization. We encouraged her to pursue this goal. But then we found out the truth. It was her own fears that prevented her from attempting anything greater.

Fear is the biggest enemy for many. It is not lack of skill that keeps people from achieving. It is lack of confidence. It is lack of faith. And as a result, they don't try to improve their lives. Faith and confidence over time can help you overcome fear. In time this talented woman began taking risks. Within months after beginning her commissioned sales job, she had doubled her income. Later, when discussing it she explained that our expressed confidence in her was the primary thing that gave her the faith to try to change. That's the infectious nature of confidence and faith.—JB

---

*According to your faith be it unto you.*

—Matthew 9:29b

Faith

COACH Lombardi had a high degree of faith in God. He had been a seminary student at one time and had planned to be a priest. Afterwards he had taught and coached in Catholic high schools and college. People who knew him described Coach Lombardi as a deeply spiritual man with profound faith in himself, his team, and God.

It's extremely important to have faith in something greater than yourself. Faith in a higher power has a reciprocal relationship with self-confidence. Your faith in a higher power measures the confidence you have in yourself. This becomes reflected in confidence in a positive outcome and in turn results in greater faith. At the initial stages, your faith in a higher power may be borrowed. It may be from a cause you deeply believe in. Your faith may be the result of fervent religious beliefs, or a dramatic spiritual experience. The important aspect is to build your faith.

Take this baby step this week. Take an inventory of the confidence you have in yourself. List your inventory in your success journal. Where you find it lacking, develop plans to compensate. Take a similar inventory of the faith and confidence you have in others. If you do not have a person you have faith in, then you probably need to make a goal to find one. Similarly, do an inventory of your belief in a higher power. If you are unsure of your faith, investigate it with someone you trust, or read books on the subject. Tapes and seminars are available to help you develop this component of your life. Author Dr. Wayne Dyer says you're not a physical being having a spiritual experience but a spiritual being having a physical experience. Agree with him or not, the fact you have spiritual needs cannot be denied. This was a part of Coach Lombardi. And it's a part of you. Nurture it, and you will be on the path to success.

---

*Faith is not belief without proof, but trust without reservations.*
—Elton True Blood

# Spirituality

SPIRITUALITY (spir´i-choo-al´e-te) n. 1. The state, quality, or fact of being spiritual. From the Latin word *spiritus* and *spirare* which translates roughly to the equivalent of "the breath of God." 2. The breath of God flowed like a river through Coach Lombardi. But he didn't preach it. He lived it. Coach Lombardi displayed his spirituality throughout his life, and believed, *well lived is far better than well said.*

Francis Cardinal Spellman is quoted as saying, "Pray as if everything depends on God, and work as if everything depends upon man." Spirituality is not something you wear. Just as wearing a Packers' jersey doesn't make you a football player, quoting the Bible does not make you spiritual. True spirituality is found in how you live and relate to your fellow man. Coach Lombardi said his priorities were God, family, and the Packers—in that order. Living it, however, was the hard part. But saying it did make it a goal and is an important part of the process.

To measure spirituality, look at the fruits of your lifestyle. Do you love people? Do you find yourself willing to love and sacrifice for others? Do others feel the breath of God through you? When the army officer told a priest he wanted to be a Catholic like Vince Lombardi, it wasn't from anything the coach had said. It came from the spiritual life he had led. As we have said many times in this book, Coach Lombardi was not perfect. He was a man who fell short of his ideals at times, as we all do. But he made his impact. And he did so by living as close to his ideals as anyone probably could. You do the same. It's a major baby step on the road to success.—VL, Jr.

---

*I derived my strength from daily mass and communion.*
—Coach Lombardi to Father Burke, St. Norbert

Spirituality

OVER the years I've met many successful people. In fact, I have met more than a few in psychotherapy. Success and wealth do not solve all your problems. In some ways in fact, success and wealth generate an entire new category of difficulties. One of the differences, however, is successful people seem more willing to open their lives to the healing power of personal development.

I have found successful people have uniquely different personalities. But there is one characteristic they all seem to share. High achievers, generally speaking, are deeply spiritual. The breath of God flows through them all. And it flows vigorously. These people are usually religious in the traditional sense of the term. Those who aren't still have a deep sense of spirituality and commitment. Few of them boast of their belief system, or use it to intimidate or impress others. It's usually an unassuming belief system and one of profound depth.

The spirituality of high achievers leaves its mark on others. They are generous, kind, and unassuming. They are willing to offer help to others and you find them becoming involved in altruistic causes. They may be wealthy, but you usually would never guess it. Universally, they are nonjudgmental of others and usually quite patient. They do make more mistakes than others. That's because they usually do more than other people. They are humble, loving, and usually peaceful. They are often misunderstood, frequently misjudged, and constantly misplacing their car keys! That's because they're involved in a greater calling and meaningfully busy doing other important things. I'm married to one. Her name is Shannon. Incidentally, if you find her car keys, please write. Thanks.—JB

---

*And why call ye me, Lord, Lord, and do not the things which I say?*
—Luke 6:46

## Spirituality

THROUGHOUT my life I've been blessed to be associated with some wonderful friends. I have discussed several of them in this book. Some I've mentioned by name. Others have asked to remain anonymous and I have respected their request.

I have often spoken about the supernatural spiritual force that is responsible for bringing souls together. This was certainly true in the case of my wife and me. I believe the same is true with Vince and our collaboration on this book. There's truly no rational reason for the basis of some people meeting. Nowhere is this more true than in the case of Carol, Ben and me.

Carol and Ben Rogers are my friends. We have collaborated on several projects. Carol, out of love, helps with the publicity and editing of my books (except for this page). And frankly, Ben and Carol have bailed me out of more than one complicated mess I've gotten myself into. They are both deeply religious people. The breath of God flows through them. I didn't say they were perfect. God doesn't hold his breath waiting for perfection. He uses you and me. He has definitely used Ben and Carol. They have been able to help countless people. And they have done so selflessly. When I go out in front of an audience to speak I often receive a standing ovation. Ben and Carol don't get the ovation. But I literally wouldn't be there today if it weren't for them. My name is on the front of this book. But it's Ben and Carol who made much of it possible. They get little attention. But they deserve unspeakable gratitude. The breath of God flows through them. It's quiet. It's like the wind. You seldom notice it. But it's always there—in people like Ben and Carol Rogers.—JB

---

*Do all the good you can, In all the ways you can, In all the places you can, To all the people you can, As long as you can.*
—John Wesley

## Spirituality

IT'S easy to be legalistic. I have often thought life would be a lot easier if God simply sent me a daily computer printout. "Do 1-17 sequentially and everything will be fine." It would simplify things. But I'm not sure any spirituality would be necessary with that approach. I would be a good robot if I followed the list, but that's not our nature. It's not possible to cultivate spirituality by following a check list.

For the breath of God to flow through you, human choices are necessary. We have discussed many of these choices in this book. Each chapter represents choices on the road to success. Faith, balance, focus, and many others are all parts of a spiritual life. The topic of the last chapter—courage—is necessary as well. It's much easier to give up and be a cynic than it is to take the path of developing spirituality. If you make this choice, you may be curious as to how it will benefit you. It's easy. You will find peace of mind as a result of living your true nature. As Wayne Dyer has said, "You're not a human being leading a spiritual life. You are a spiritual being leading a human life."

Take this baby step today. Begin evaluating your spiritual life. When the breath of God attempts to flow through you, welcome it. Perhaps in the past you have been frightened of it. Maybe you have run and hid. Many times we simply ignore it. Or perhaps you're still searching. Talk to someone you trust or respect. It could be a friend or clergy. Perhaps it's someone you really don't know yet, but who has impressed you with their peacefulness. Take some risks. Tell the person you want to buy him or her lunch and talk about spirituality. Examine books and tapes to help you investigate your spiritual life. It's a baby step on the road to success.

---

*If you pray for bread and bring no basket to carry it, you prove the doubting spirit which may be the only hindrance to the gift you ask.*
—D. L. Moody

# Courage

COURAGE (kur´ij) n. 1. The state of mind or spirit that enables one to face opposition with self-possession, confidence, and resolution. 2. Coach Lombardi was diagnosed with cancer on Memorial Day weekend, 1970. He was buried on Labor Day weekend. At 57 years of age, at the pinnacle of fame and achievement, he seemed both too young and too powerful to die. Yet he didn't lament what was happening to him. Rather he accepted it with grace and just a touch of wistfulness. As he told a priest who often visited him near the end, "I'm not afraid to die, but there are many things I haven't accomplished yet."

Courage, contrary to current thought, is not the absence of fear. Popular culture, reflected in films featuring some male macho-muscle star, would give you the impression that to succeed you must be fearless. "Don't let them see you sweat," is the word for today. Nothing could be further from the truth. If you don't occasionally experience fear, tension, or anxiety, check your pulse. You might be dead. Courage is experiencing fear, recognizing it for what it is, and then if it's important enough, pushing ahead in spite of your fear.

I'm fearful every time I get ready to speak. My heart beats faster. I feel a rush of adrenaline. I visit the men's room with increased frequency. But I welcome the feeling. It's a good indication I'm ready. Yes, I could forget what I plan to say, or the audience might not like me or my message. I could bomb! I've bombed before. All these thoughts make me fearful. But the goal is powerful. In spite of my fear, I muster the courage to get up and speak. My goal is stronger than my fear. Courage is not in being macho. It's in doing your work, regardless of your fear.—VL, Jr.

---

*Winning is not everything—but making the effort to win is.*
—Coach Lombardi

## Courage

THERE are many things I respect about Coach Lombardi. One of the most profound is his understanding of the typical cycle of success. Most people reach a peak of achievement and rapidly fall back to the status quo. It is doubtless far more difficult to repeat success than to initially achieve it. Unlike most people, Coach Lombardi had the unique ability to stretch out the life cycle of the Packers' success.

Numerous factors contribute to the downfall of a hero. I discussed many of them in *The Elvis Syndrome,* and will cover others in its sequel. There is one factor, however, that stands above them all. It's courage. It takes unfathomable degrees of courage to remain at the peak level of achievement. The easier choice is to achieve and then rest on your laurels. You've "made" it. It requires less energy and work. You no longer have to risk failure. Fewer people will be uncomfortable with you. Little or no courage is required.

The list of high-achievers who self-sabotage or simply give up is unbelievably long. As one philosopher said, ". . . Show me a hero, I'll tell you a tragedy. . ." From King David in the Old Testament to O.J. Simpson in 1997, the list lengthens annually. Some would say it's a death wish. Others claim it's sowing what you reap. In some cases perhaps both are true. In most cases I've investigated, it's neither. It's lack of courage. Rising once you fall, as Coach Lombardi discussed, is important. But rising before you fall further is equally important. Prevention is definitely more important than cure in this particular case. Realize this and learn from it. The stress of success is far worse than the stress of failure. You will need courage to face it. Get prepared and don't give in to the status quo of mediocrity.—JB

---

*Courage is resistance to fear, mastery of fear—not absence of fear.*
                                                                —Mark Twain

## Courage

IT has been my complete honor to collaborate with Vince Lombardi, Jr. on this book inspired by his dad, the coach. We have spent a lot of time on the phone and more that a few hours sitting across from each other discussing success, family, and life in general. I have met one of his sons, and look forward to meeting the rest of his family. Vince is a brilliant man, and obviously has been an involved husband and parent. I respect those qualities.

During the time we've worked on this project I have also grown to speculate about how difficult it must be to be the only son of an icon and actually bear his name. Other than John F. Kennedy, I'm not sure there's anyone currently well-known who's footsteps would be more difficult to follow. But Vince has carved out what I see as his own identity and displayed the kind of courage few comprehend. Frankly, what could he do for an encore? You can't compete with a legend of mythical proportions. So what *do* you do?

Many people give up. Others find solace in alcohol, drugs, or depression. Some live off royalties or trust funds and squander it away. Any of these alternatives are easy. They don't require even a small degree of courage. Vince has chosen a different approach. His life work, similar to his father's, has been helping people improve their lives. But he does it through speaking. I personally know it's not an easy life. Vince doesn't enjoy living out of hotels or flying three to five days a week. But by doing so he has helped thousands of people. It's not an easy choice for him. But he has a gift. So he makes the courageous choice. To open himself up in this book was also not an easy choice. But it was the courageous one. His impact on my life and the lives of others has only begun to be appreciated. Yes, Coach Lombardi was a phenomenon. But his son Vince is a hero as well. I can't help but believe the coach would issue a gap-toothed smile and say, "That's my boy. I'm proud of him."—JB

---

*Fear none of those things which thou shalt suffer.*
—Revelation 2:10a

Courage
---

IT takes courage to stand up for what you believe. A simple psychological study done years ago illustrates this point. In this study three straight lines were drawn on a chalk board. One line was clearly longer than the other two. It did require a small degree of discrimination but by taking a close inspection you could clearly distinguish the longer line from the others. A group of students were taught to cooperate in the study by misidentifying one of the obviously shorter lines as being the longest. The last student, the only one who really didn't understand what was going on, was then asked to choose the longest line. This student would invariably agree with the others. He would choose the same line everyone else had even though it was clearly the wrong one.

It takes an unusual brand of courage to be different. In fact, it's extremely difficult to be different—even if different is right. Peer pressure, the need for acceptance, and concern about being labeled as an outsider, make most people avoid being different. Unfortunately, this is true, even if *different* means being successful. This is so true that most people will even deny the obvious to avoid making choices that are unpopular. It's no wonder that drug use is so prevalent among peer groups. If rising above the mediocre requires your being different, it will take the kind of courage most people don't have. Get ready for it. If you overcome this problem you will be among the few who experience truly extraordinary success.

Take this baby step today. If this is the first time you have read this book, read it again. Do it slowly and comprehensively. Study and understand it. Digest it. If this is your second reading, congratulations! Now form a study group. Be courageous. You volunteer to be the leader. Order workbooks and other study material. We believe if you read this book twice and lead two different study groups you will not only experience success, you will have the courage to remain successful over the long term.

---

*Life is either a daring adventure or nothing.*

—Helen Keller

# Epilogue

EPILOGUE (ep´e-log) n. 1. A short addition or concluding section at the end of any literary work, often dealing with the future of its characters. 2. This is the epilogue. It's written after the manuscript has been completed and there has been time to think about the book. Some might say it's been an ambitious undertaking. It does take a little "brass" to think this book can add anything to the thousands of other self-help books. But you have read thus far. And that's why we wrote it—for you.

As we look back on this book, one thing is clearly evident. Success, growth, and self-improvement is a *process*. It doesn't just happen. You don't leave it to chance. You weren't born with or without it. It's really a series of things you do. And more importantly, it's a way of thinking. If success and improved performance are important to you then there is a certain body of knowledge you must possess.

Successful people know this information. Interestingly enough, they may not even know they know it! It's like riding a bicycle. By practicing the principles of bike riding for awhile it eventually becomes automatic. You don't have to think, ". . . Balance; lean; turn; pedal; balance . . ." You just do it. It's the same with successful people. They don't have to concentrate on principles one through fifty-two. They live them. If you spend enough time around people you consider high performers, you will notice certain things. Certain basic thought patterns will begin to become apparent to you. And it's those thought patterns we have presented here. Study them. Read them. Learn them. Become them. And then ride the bicycle of success.

---

*Hold your head high, stick your chest out. You can make it. It gets dark sometimes but morning comes.*
—Reverend Jesse Jackson

## Epilogue

A quotable Roman by the name of Marcus Aurelius said, "The art of living is more like wrestling than dancing." Life is difficult. It comes to us in a series of challenges. To present life as anything else is a disservice. It's not the challenges that destroy you, however. Your mindset is the culprit. Your mindset will determine whether your life will be rewarding or not.

Victor Frankl was a famous Austrian psychotherapist who spent most of WWII in a concentration camp. He lost his wife, child, and his life's work during incarceration. But as time passed he became fascinated with how some people quickly perished and others actually grew stronger. Yet they all faced similar, if not the same, hardships. After years of observation and reflection Frankl drew a number of conclusions.

Part of the answer he surmised had to do with attitude. Each individual's perception of their situation was at least as important as the situation itself. His observations were summed up with some profound statements. "Everything can be taken from a man but one thing, the last of human freedoms, the ability to choose one's own way." Some chose the way of giving up. It would be understandable. Yet others chose not only to survive but to help others. Frankl himself, decided not only to live, but to find meaning in the tragedy. He decided to survive and dedicate his life to ensuring nothing like the holocaust would ever happen again. "The art of living is more like wrestling than dancing." The wrestling won't destroy you. But your attitude will. Find meaning in your struggles. Don't give up. Choose your own way—the way of success.

---

*God doesn't require us to succeed; he only requires that you try.*
—Mother Teresa

## Epilogue

*THE will to win and achieve goes dry and arid without constant reinforcement.* There is a major trap you need to avoid. It's an easy one to fall into, so be careful. You might hear or see something that inspires you and you come to believe you've got "it." And then you move on. Some people may respond to this book in the same manner. You might read a page, or perhaps just a quote. You think you've got it. And then you forget it.

Throughout history the people we call successful have all had times that could be called their *desert experiences*. They had been confused and discouraged. But they didn't give up. The reason was because of their propensity to turn to "constant reinforcement." They needed it. So do you.

This is not the kind of material you can read once and expect a life change to occur. Don't just read about these principles. Digest them. There is little in this book that can be referred to as original. You can find similar ideas in the Bible, Shakespeare, or Emerson. We authors have simply organized it and said it in a different way. And if you have gotten this far, we have obviously communicated to you. Now there's another important baby step for you to take. You need to constantly reinforce these ideas. Read the book again. Watch videos. Listen to tapes. Finish the workbook. Go to a seminar. Sooner or later, through this process of constant reinforcement, you will begin to internalize the habits, beliefs, and thought patterns of successful people. Then, when faced with your next challenge, you will react instinctively. And your instinct will be successful.—VL, Jr.

---

*The ultimate victory can never be completely won. Yet it must be pursued with all one's might.*

—**Coach Lombardi**

VINCE LOMBARDI, JR. is an author and speaker with a clear and inspiring message to share about the qualities and commitment found in high performance people and organizations! His message stems from a lifetime of experience and observation.

As the son of the late Vincent T. Lombardi, one of the greatest football coaches in the history of the sport, Vince's early years were spent in an atmosphere full of personal power and achievement. Armed with honesty, integrity, and authenticity, virtues he places above all others, Vince earned a law degree and maintained a private practice while serving in the Minnesota legislature.

Vince made the jump from law and politics to professional football in 1975 when he joined the fledgling Seattle Seahawks as Assistant to the General Manager. He went on to become Assistant Executive Director of the National Football League Management Council as a labor negotiator and later led two United States Football League teams as President and General Manager.

To each of these organizations Vince brought direction, enthusiasm, and the impetus to succeed. He has the remarkable ability to put people ahead of the organization, allowing each individual to do what he does best without losing sight of team goals. He gained a reputation for being tough, yet fair; uncompromising, yet supportive. The individual qualities and character of Vince Lombardi are exciting to witness.

Vince's book, *Coaching for Teamwork: Winning Concepts for Business in the Twenty-First Century*, is an inspiring book of concepts for achieving excellence through teamwork. It is an invaluable tool for helping people evaluate management skills, goals, and vision and establish a blueprint for going successfully into the future.

Vince is a compelling public speaker who provides his audiences with vital tools for improved performance. He inspires his listeners to lasting positive growth and personal excellence. It is an emotional uplift to watch and listen as Vince weaves together his childhood experiences with his father and his adult experiences from law, politics, and professional football. Vince's enthusiasm for growth, change, and improved performance, blended with his strong personality and first-hand knowledge of his legendary father's leadership and teambuilding techniques, provides for a dynamic presentation.

To book Vince Lombardi as a speaker please call 1-800-736-6196.

DR. JOHN BAUCOM was once introduced by Howard Cosell as the world's leading authority on the unique problems of high achievers. John has been writing, consulting, speaking, and giving radio and television interviews for years about the challenges facing high achievers.

An expert in human performance, he can come on site within an organization and work with high performers individually or in groups. This is done through consultations, seminars, training sessions, and as a keynote speaker. He helps companies increase productivity, improve customer loyalty, and contribute to the bottom line through strengthening its people. He specializes in pragmatic solutions customized to each individual client's needs. John combines the training and credibility of a doctoral-level education with the experiential base of a former college teacher and Department of Defense Advisor in human relations and leadership.

One of the few experts who writes about this subject, John has shared the speaker's podium with such notables as Surgeon General C. Everett Koop, Senator Bill Bradley, Howard Cosell, comedian Jerry Clower, and many others. He has been heard in Japan, Germany, Great Britain, Russia and on countless broadcasts nationally including *Good Morning America, Sally Jessy Raphael, Hour Magazine, The Jim Bohannon Show, CNN Headline News*. Additionally, he has been interviewed with Regis Philben, Joan Lunden, Zig Ziglar, and Larry King.

John is a former Marine Corps officer and paratrooper who spent two tours of combat duty in Vietnam. He is the recipient of various decorations including the Silver Star, Bronze Star, and Vietnamese Cross of Gallantry. During his combat experience he served as an advisor to the native Montagnard and Mung tribesmen indigenous to Vietnam, Laos, and Cambodia.

Today, John describes his specialty this way. ". . . You know how textbooks discuss the life cycle of a product? What I specialize in is the life cycle of your success. There are ways to avoid self-sabotage, burnout, or dying young. My passion is to help achievers balance their lives and experience long-term peak performance. You really can achieve professional success, individual fulfillment, and live a long productive life. You just need the right road map. . . ."

To book Dr. John Baucom as a speaker or consultant please call toll free: 1-888-899-8331.

# Bibliography & Resource Section

Baucom, John Q., *Baby Steps to Happiness:52 Inspiring Ways to Make Your Life Happy.* Pennsylvania: Starburst Publishers, 1996.

Baucom, John Q., *Little Baby Steps to Happiness: Inspiring Quotes and Affirmations to Make Your Life Happy.* Pennsylvania: Starburst Publishers, 1996.

Baucom, John Q., *The Elvis Syndrome: How to Avoid Death by Success.* Minneapolis: Fairview Press, 1995.

Baucom, John Q., *The Zelda Complex: How to Avoid Toxic Relationships.* Minneapolis: Fairview Press, 1996.

Baucom, John Q., and Barry Wagner, *The Little ABC's of Balance: How to Live Successfully and Avoid Burnout!* Chattanooga: LA Press, 1997.

Blanchard, Ken. *One Minute Manager.* New York: Berkley, 1994.

Bland, Glenn. *Success: The Glenn Bland Method.* Wheaton, IL: Tyndale House Publishers, Inc., 1972.

Buscaglia, Leo. *Bus 9 To Paradise.* New York: Ballantine Books, 1986.

Cousins, Norman. *Anatomy of an Illness as Perceived by the Patient.* New York: W. W. Norton & Co., Inc., 1979.

Covey, Stephen R. *The 7 Habits of Highly Effective People.* New York: Simon & Schuster, Inc., 1990.

Covey, Stephen and Rebecca Merrill. *First Things First.* New York: Simon & Schuster, 1996.

Didinger, Ray, ed. *Game Plans For Success.* New York: Little, Brown and Company, 1995.

Dyer, Wayne. *The Sky's The Limit.* New York: Pocket Books, 1980.

Dyer, Wayne. *Your Erroneous Zones.* New York: Harper & Row Publishers, Inc., 1976.

Frankl, Viktor E. *Man's Search For Meaning.* New York: Pocket Books, 1973.

Griessman, B. Eugene. *Time Tactics of Very Successful People.* New York: McGraw-Hill, Inc., 1994.

Hill, Napoleon. *The Master Key to Riches.* New York: Fawcett Crest Books, 1965.

Hill, Napoleon. *Think and Grow Rich.* New York: Penguin Books, 1988.

Hill, Napoleon, and W. Clement Stone. *Success Through A Positive Mental Attitude.* Englewood Cliffs, NJ: Prentice-Hall, Inc., 1977.

Horino, Midori. "The Relation Between Achievement Motive and Fear of Success." *The Japanese Journal of Psychology*, October 1991, 62:255-259.

James, Muriel, and Dorothy Jongeward. *Born to Win.* New York: Penguin Books USA, Inc., 1971.

James, William. *The Philosophy of William James.* comp. Horace M. Kalen. New York: Randam House, 1961.

James, William. *The Varieties of Religious Experience.* New York: The Modern Library-Randam House, 1902.

Lombardi, Vince. *Coaching for Teamwork: Winning Concepts for Business in the Twenty-First Century.* Washington: Reinforcement Press, 1996

Maltz, Maxwell, M.D. *Creative Living Today.* New York: Simon & Schuster, Inc., 1967.

Maltz, Maxwell, M.D. *Psycho-Cybernetics.* New Jersey: Pocket Books, 1987.

Maltz, Maxwell, M.D. *The Search For Self-Respect.* New York: Grosset & Dunlap, Inc., 1973.

Mandino, Og. *Og Mandino's University of Success.* New York: Bantam Books, 1982.

Musashi, Miyamoto. *A Book Of Five Rings,* trans. Victor Harris. Woodstock, NY: The Overlook Press, 1974.

Oates, Bob, Jr. *The Winner's Edge.* Fairfield, IA: Christopher, Mallay, and Co., 1980.

Peale, Norman Vincent. *You Can If You Think You Can.* New York: Fawcett Crest Books, 1974.

Peck, M. Scott. *The Road Less Traveled.* New York: Simon & Schuster, Inc., 1978.

Peters, Tom. *In Search of Excellence.* New York: Little, Brown & Co., 1984.

Peters, Tom. *Thriving on Chaos: Handbook for a Management Revolution.* New York: Alfred A. Knopf, Inc., 1987.

Qubein, Nido R. *Stairway to Success.* Mechanicsburg, PA: Executive Books, 1996.

Qubein, Nido R. *Achieving Peak Performance.* Minneapolis: Best Sellers Publishing, 1996.

Ries, Al, *Focus.* New York: Harper Collins, 1996.

Robbins, Anthony. *Awaken the Giant Within.* New York: Simon & Schuster, 1992.

Scott, Steven K. *A Millionaire's Notebook.* New York: Simon & Schuster, 1996.

Tarkenton, Fran. *Playing to Win: Fran Tarkenton's Strategies for Business Success.* New York: Harper & Row Publishers, Inc., 1984.

Thoreau, Henry David. *Walden.* New York: The Heritage Press, 1939.

Ward, Baldwin H., ed. *The Great Innovators.* New York: Year, Inc., 1970.

Whitman, Howard. *Success is Within You.* New York: Doubleday & Co., Inc., 1956.

Ziglar, Zig. *See You At The Top.* Gretna, LA: Pelican Publishing Company, Inc., 1983.

## Books About Coach Lombardi

Klein, Dave. *The Vince Lombardi Story.* New York: Lion Books, 1971.

Lombardi, *Vince. Run to Daylight.* Englewood Cliffs, NJ: Prentice-Hall, Inc. 1963.

O'Brien, Michael. *Vince: A Personal Biography of Vince Lombardi.* New York; William Morrow and Company, Inc. 1987.

Schoor, Gene. *Football's Greatest Coach: Vince Lombardi.* Garden City, NY: Doubleday & Co., Inc., 1974.

Wiebusch, John, ed. *Lombardi.* Chicago: Follett Publishing Company, 1971.

## Quotes

Anderson, Peggy, ed. *Great Quotes From Great Women.* Lombard, IL: Successories Publishing, 1992

Curtis Management Group, ed. *Motivation Lombardi Style.* Lombard, IL: Successories Publishing, 1992.

Davis, Wynn, ed. *The Best of Success.* Lombard, IL: Great Quotations Publishing Company, 1988.

Emerson, Ralph Waldo. "Self-Reliance." in *Major Writers of America.* ed. Newton Arvin. New York: Harcourt, Brace & World, Inc., 1966.

Ferguson, Howard E. *The Edge.* Cleveland, OH: Getting the Edge Company, 1990.

Henry, Lewis C., ed. *Five Thousand Quotations For All Occasions.* New York: Doubleday & Company, Inc., 1975.

Merriam-Webster, ed. *The Merriam Dictionary of Quotations.* Springfield, MA: Merriam Webster, Inc., 1992.

Morris, William, ed. et al. *The American Heritage Dictionary.* New York: American Heritage Publishing Co., 1969.

Newfelott, Victoria, and David B. Guralnick, ed. *Webster's New World Dictionary.* New York: Simon & Schuster, Inc., 1988.

Peter, Laurence J., ed. Peter's Quotations. New York: Bantam Books, 1977.

Princeton Language Institute, ed. *21st Century Dictionary of Quotations.* New York: Philip Lief Group, Inc., 1993.

Rawson, Hugh, and Margaret Miner, ed. *The New International Dictionary of Quotations.* New York: E. P. Dutton, 1986.

Safire, William, and Leonard Safire, ed. *Good Advice.* New York: Wing Books, 1992.

Seldes, George, ed. *The Great Thoughts.* New York: Ballantine Books, 1966.

Simcox, Carol E., ed. *Four Thousand and Five Hundred Quotations For Christian Communicators.* Grand Rapids, MI: Baker Book House, 1992.

Sweeting, George, ed. *Who Said That?* Chicago: Moody Press, 1995.

Tyndale House Publishers. *The Living Bible.* Wheaton, IL: Tyndale House Publishers, 1981.

Warner, Carolyn, ed. *The Last Word: A Treasury of Women's Quotes.* Englewood Cliffs, NJ: Prentice Hall, 1992.

Zondervan Publishing House. *Women's Devotional Bible: New International Version.* Grand Rapids, MI: Zondervan Corporation, 1990.

## Tapes

Many of the books listed above are on tape and are available at your local bookstore or through Nightingale-Conant Corporation, 7300 North Lehigh Avenue, Chicago, IL 60648 1-800-323-5552.

## Time Management Systems

Day-Timers, Inc. 1-800-452-7398

Franklin Covey Co. 1-800-654-1776

Geodex International, Inc., 1-800-833-3030

# Index

# Books by Starburst Publishers
(Partial listing—full list available on request)

**Baby Steps to Success** —Vince Lombardi Jr. & John Q. Baucom

Subtitled: *52 Vince Lombardi-Inspired Ways to Make Your Life Successful.* Vince Lombardi's is one of the most quoted success stories in the history of the world. From corporate boardrooms to athletic locker rooms, his wisdom is studied, read, and posted on walls. The same skills that Coach Lombardi used to turn the Green Bay Packers from cellar dwellers to world champions is now available to you in *Baby Steps To Success.* This book can help you be more successful in your career, personal or family life. The same principles that made the Packers Super Bowl champions can make you a "Super Bowl" employee, parent or spouse. These principles are broken down into 52 unique and achievable "Baby Steps."

(trade paper) ISBN: 0914984950 **$12.95**

**"Little" Baby Steps to Success** —Vince Lombardi Jr. & John Q. Baucom

Subtitled: *Vince Lombardi-Inspired Motivational Wisdom & Insight to Make Your Life Successful.* Motivational, inspiring and filled with insight that will get you off the bench and into the game of success. This wisdom-filled, pocket-sized collection of the best of Lombardi will help you one small step at a time to reach the goals you have imagined.

(trade paper) ISBN: 0914984969 **$6.95**

**Baby Steps to Happiness** —John Q. Baucom

Subtitled: *52 Inspiring Ways to Make Your Life Happy.* This unique 52-step approach will enable the reader to focus on small steps that bring practical and proven change. The author encourages the reader to take responsibility for the Happiness that only he can find. Chapter titles, such as, *Have a Reason to Get Out of Bed, Deal with Your Feelings or Become Them, Would You Rather Be Right or Happy?*, and *Love To Win More Than You Hate to Lose* give insight and encouragement on the road to happiness.

(trade paper) ISBN 0914984861 **$12.95**

**Little Baby Steps to Happiness** —John Q. Baucom

Subtitled: *Inspiring Quotes and Affirmations to Make Your Life Happy.* Inspiring, witty and insightful, this portable collection of quotes and affirmations from *Baby Steps to Happiness* will encourage Happiness one little footstep at a time. This book is the perfect personal "cheerleader."

(trade paper) ISBN 091498487X **$6.95**

**Winning At Golf** —David A. Smith

Addresses the growing needs of aspiring young golfers yearning for correct instruction, positive guidance, and discipline. It is an attempt not only to increase the reader's knowledge of the swing, but also sets forth to inspire and motivate the reader to a new and rewarding way of life. *Winning At Golf* relays the teachings of Buck White, the author's mentor and a tour winner many times over. It gives instruction to the serious golfer and challenges the average golfer to excel.

(trade paper) ISBN 0914984462 **$9.95**

**Lease–Purchase America!** —John Ross

A first-of-its-kind book that provides a simple "nuts and bolts" approach to acquiring real estate. Explains how the lease-purchase technique pioneered by John Ross can now be used in real estate to more easily buy and sell a home. Details the value of John's technique from the perspective of each participant in the real estate transaction. Illustrates how the reader can use lease-purchase successfully as a tool to achieve his or her real estate goals.

(trade paper) ISBN 0914984454 **$9.95**

## More Books by Starburst Publishers

**Migraine—Winning The Fight of Your Life**                    —Charles Theisler

This book describes the hurt, loneliness and agony that migraine sufferers experience and the difficulty they must live with. It explains the different types of migraines and their symptoms, as well as the related health hazards. Gives 200 ways to help fight off migraines, and shows how to experience fewer headaches, reduce their duration, and decrease the agony and pain involved.

(trade paper)  ISBN 0914984632  **$10.95**

**The Crystal Clear Guide to Sight for Life**                    —Gayton & Ledford

Subtitled: *A Complete Manual of Eye Care for Those Over 40. The Crystal Clear Guide to Sight For Life* makes eye care easy-to-understand by giving clear knowledge of how the eye works with the most up-to-date information available from the experts. Contains more than 40 illustrations, a detailed index for cross-referencing, a concise glossary, and answers often-asked questions. This book takes much of the guesswork out of eye problems, alleviating fear and apprehension often experienced by patients when medical problems develop.

(trade paper)  ISBN 0914984683  **$15.95**

**Home Business Happiness**                    —Cheri Fuller

Subtitled: *Secrets On Keeping The Family Ship Afloat From Entrepreneurs Who Made It.* More than 26 million people in the U.S. work at home businesses. *Home Business Happiness* is your network for success! In a reader-friendly style. Author Cheri Fuller offers valuable advice from some of the most inventive and pioneering entrepreneurs in the country. Some of the topics included are: Starting a Home Business, Time Management, and Avoiding Potential Pitfalls.

(trade paper)  ISBN 0914984705  **$12.95**

**God's Abundance**                    —Edited by Kathy Miller

This day-by-day inspirational is a collection of thoughts by leading Christian writers such as, Patsy Clairmont, Jill Briscoe, Liz Curtis Higgs and Naomi Rhode. God's Abundance is based on God's Word for a simpler, yet more abundant life. Similar in style to the best-seller, Simple Abundance, but with a Biblical basis. Most people think more about the future while the present passes through their hands. Learn to make all aspects of your life—personal, business, financial, relationships, even housework be a "spiritual abundance of simplicity."

(hard cover)  ISBN 0914984977  **$19.95**

**Revelation—God's Word for the Biblically-Inept**                    —Daymond Duck

*Revelation—God's Word for the Biblically-Inept* is the first in a new series designed to make understanding and learning the Bible as easy and fun as learning your ABC's. Reading the Bible is one thing, understanding it is another! This book breaks down the barrier of difficulty and helps take the Bible off the pedestal and into your hands.

(trade paper)  ISBN 0914984985  **$16.95**

**God's Vitamin "C" for the Spirit**                    —Kathy Collard Miller & D. Larry Miller

Subtitled: *"Tug-at-the-Heart" Stories to Fortify and Enrich Your Life.* Includes inspiring stories and anecdotes that emphasize Christian ideals and values by Barbara Johnson, Billy Graham, Nancy L. Dorner, Dave Dravecky, Patsy Clairmont, Charles Swindoll and many other well-known Christian speakers and writers. Topics include: Love, Family Life, Faith and Trust, Prayer and God's Guidance.

(trade paper)  ISBN 0914984837  **$12.95**

## More Books by Starburst Publishers

**God's Chewable Vitamin "C" for the Spirit**

Subtitled: *A Dose of God's Wisdom One Bite at a Time.* A collection of inspirational quotes and Scriptures by many of your favorite Christian speakers and writers. It will motivate your life and inspire your spirit. You will *chew* on every *bite* of *God's Chewable Vitamin "C" for the Spirit.*

(trade paper) ISBN 0914984845 **$6.95**

**God's Vitamin "C" for the Spirit of MEN** —D. Larry Miller

Subtitled: *"Tug-at-the-Heart" Stories to Encourage and Strengthen Your Spirit.* This book is filled with unique and inspiring stories that men of all ages will immediately relate to.

(trade paper) ISBN 0914984810 **$12.95**

**God's Chewable Vitamin "C" for the Spirit of DADs**

Subtitled: *A Dose of Godly Character, One Bite at a Time.* Scriptures coupled with insightful quotes to inspire men through the changes of life.

(trade paper) ISBN 0914984829 **$6.95**

**God's Vitamin "C" for the Spirit of WOMEN** —Kathy Collard Miller

Subtitled: *"Tug-at-the Heart"* stories to Inspire and Delight Your Spirit. A beautiful treasury of timeless stories, quotes and poetry designed by and for women. Well-known Christian women like Liz Curtis Higgs, Patsy Clairmont, Naomi Rhode and Elisabeth Elliott share from their hearts on subjects like Marriage, Motherhood, Christian Living, Faith and Friendship.

(trade paper) ISBN 0914984934 **$12.95**

**God's Chewable Vitamin "C" for the Spirit of MOMs**

Delightful, Insightful and Inspirational quotes combined with Scriptures that uplift and encourage women to succeed at the most important job in life—Motherhood.

(trade paper) ISBN 0914984942 **$6.95**

**God's Vitamin "C" for the Christmas Spirit** —Kathy Collard Miller & D. Larry Miller

Subtitled: *"Tug-at-the-Heart" Traditions and Inspirations to Warm the Heart.* This keepsake includes a variety of heart-tugging thoughts, stories, poetry, recipes, songs and crafts.

(hardcover) ISBN 0914984853 **$14.95**

**God's Vitamin "C" for the Hurting Spirit**

The latest in the best-selling *God's Vitamin "C" for the Spirit* series, this collection of real-life stories expresses the breadth and depth of God's love for us in our times of need. Rejuvenating and inspiring thoughts from some of the most-loved Christian writers such as Max Lucado, Cynthia Heald, Charles Swindoll and Barbara Johnson. Topics include: Death, Divorce/Separation, Financial Loss and Physical Illness.

(trade paper) ISBN 0914984691 **$12.95**

**The Miracle of the Sacred Scroll** —Johan Christian

In this poignant book, Johan Christian masterfully weaves historical and Biblical reality together with a touching fictional story to bring to life this marvelous work—a story that takes its main character, Simon of Cyrene, on a journey which transforms his life, and that of the reader, from one of despair and defeat to success and triumph!

(hardcover) ISBN 091498473X **$14.95**

## Purchasing Information:

Books are available from your favorite Bookstore, either from current stock or special order. To assist bookstore in locating your selection be sure to give title, author, and ISBN #. If unable to purchase from the bookstore you may order direct from STARBURST PUBLISHERS. When ordering enclose full payment plus $3.00 for shipping and handling ($4.00 if Canada or Overseas). Payment in US Funds only. Please allow two to three weeks minimum (longer overseas) for delivery. Make checks payable to and mail to STARBURST PUBLISHERS, P.O. Box 4123, LANCASTER, PA 17604. Credit card orders may also be placed by calling 1-800-441-1456 (credit card orders only), Mon-Fri, 8:30 a.m. – 5:30 p.m. Eastern Time. **Prices subject to change without notice.** Catalog available for a 9 x 12 self-addressed envelope with 4 first-class stamps.    9-97